W9-BVP-387

What's Gaby Cooking

EVERYDAY CALIFORNIA FOOD

Editor: Holly Dolce
Designer: Claudia Wu
Production Manager: Denise LaCongo

Library of Congress Control Number: 2017945293

ISBN: 978-1-4197-2894-5
eISBN: 978-1-68335-220-4

Printed and bound in China
10 9 8 7 6 5 4 3 2 1

ABRAMS The Art of Books
195 Broadway, New York, NY 10007
abramsbooks.com

What's Gaby Cooking

EVERYDAY CALIFORNIA FOOD

Gaby Dalkin

Photographs by Matt Armendariz

ABRAMS, NEW YORK

Contents

Introduction

Welcome to the What's Gaby Cooking world, where I'm all about living that California Girl life! For me, this sunny slice of heaven is less a state than it is a state of mind—where the name of the game is tuning into a shinier frequency, working hard but playing harder, and daydreaming about next weekend's road trip. Out here we never need much of an excuse to get together—we're into our toasts, whether they're topped with avocado (naturally) or clinking glasses of bubbly (obviously). From long-weekend cookouts to outdoor movie nights, ocean-side picnics to birthday brunches, bridal showers to cookbook clubs, for me, there's not really anything that isn't a good excuse for company and an epic spread. That's why I've dedicated this book to sharing my favorite recipes for whipping up something fresh, simple, and delicious—whether it's for two or for twenty. *What's Gaby Cooking* is all about everyday California food, it's your guide for bringing a piece of that West Coast vibe home, even if you're not a bike ride away from the beach.

No matter where you live, you can still apply the same California Girl philosophies, which means keeping things easy and carefree. It's always having something tasty to eat, thanks to handy and delicious pantry staples (coconut oil! quinoa! limes! dark chocolate!), super-fresh market treasures (whether from the grocery store or the farmers' market, there's nothing more California than a pop of color from in-season produce), as well as an arsenal of simple recipes (pick a page, any page!). It's having a rotating stock of double-duty sauces and dressings on hand (like Basil Vinaigrette and Lemon and Garlic Hummus) to drizzle, dollop, and dip. And it's definitely *not* spending all day in the kitchen.

If there's anything I've learned from my time out here, it's that perfect is overrated—unless you're talking about the perfect day to get outside, breathe in some fresh air, and hang out with friends for a few rounds of rosé and whatever's coming off the grill. Can we sometimes be a little nutty about our health? Occasionally—we haven't met a smoothie we haven't loved—but we'll also never say no to a burrito with extra guacamole. Balance is the name of the game, and the same goes for the recipes in this book. While you're nourishing your body with dishes like Green Rice Burrito Bowls, Pesto Broccolini, and Fish Tacos with Pineapple-Mango Salsa, you'll always know that a treat like Cinnamon Roll–Chocolate Chip Monkey Bread, or—of course—my favorite, Chocolate Chip S'mookies, are only a meal away.

So go ahead, get the girls (and guys) together for a day at the beach, a picnic in the park, or an outdoor pizza party. Spend a post-hike afternoon soaking up the last few hours of sunlight over a fresh, hearty meal you cobbled together from whatever you have on hand. Because whether you're hosting a crowd for a Mexi-Cali fiesta or a couple for Tuesday night dinner, these recipes will help you turn any meal into a special one. From there, the only thing left to do is kick back, make yourself a juice (and by juice I mean a pitcher of California Girl Margaritas, page 27) and listen for those ocean waves.

Getting Prepped:

Kitchen Staples

There are two key ingredients to being a good cook: 1) confidence, and 2) a well-stocked pantry. Below is a list of items I like to keep on hand at all times so I can whip up most anything in a flash. From condiments and spices to grains and flours, it's everything you need to put dinner on the table. Just add fresh produce and protein and you're on your way to a perfect California-inspired meal.

Dry Goods

Grains | Beans | Pasta

- Farro
- Quinoa
- White rice
- Brown rice
- Black beans
- Pinto beans
- Pasta (various shapes)
- Panko bread crumbs
- Regular bread crumbs

Baking Staples

- All-purpose flour
- Granulated sugar
- Oats
- Brown sugar
- Shredded coconut
- Chocolate chips
- Dark chocolate
- Agave nectar
- Cocoa powder
- Vanilla extract
- Honey
- Baking powder
- Baking soda
- Nonstick baking spray

Nuts + Seeds

- Walnuts
- Cashews
- Almonds
- Peanuts
- Chia seeds
- Almond butter
- Peanut butter

Oils

- Olive oil
- Toasted sesame oil
- Coconut oil
- Avocado oil
- Vegetable oil

Vinegars

- Red wine vinegar
- Balsamic vinegar
- White wine vinegar
- Champagne vinegar
- Apple cider vinegar
- Balsamic glaze

Condiments

- Ketchup
- Mustard
- Mayo
- Soy sauce
- Sriracha
- Tahini

Salt, Herbs, + Spices

- Maldon sea salt
- Kosher salt
- Black peppercorns
- Chili powder
- Crushed red pepper flakes
- Dried oregano
- Dried basil
- Dried thyme
- Garlic powder
- Garlic salt
- Ground cayenne
- Ground cinnamon
- Ground cumin
- Onion powder
- Paprika
- Smoked paprika

Pantry Produce

- Onions
- Garlic
- Shallots

Canned or Jarred Goods

- Canned beans
- Canned tomatoes
- Pasta sauce
- Castelvetrano olives
- Sun-dried tomatoes
- Chipotle chiles in adobo
- Chicken stock or broth
- Nut butters
- Tomato paste

Fridge Staples

- Milk
- Eggs
- Almond milk
- Butter
- Greek yogurt
- Cheese
- Lemons
- Limes
- Ginger
- Fresh herbs
- Seasonal vegetables
- Fruits
- Tortillas

Chapter 1:

Appetizers + Bites

I'm a professional snacker, so when it comes to putting out tasty bites for guests, I know what I'm doing. Having bits and bobs to munch on is the most important part of any party because they're the first thing everyone gets to try, plus it's a fun way to get everyone mixing and mingling. Whether it's fresh, cold oysters with homemade mignonette; ooey-gooey queso; an epic cheese board; or any salty, sweet, tangy, crunchy, chewy nosh in between, I've got you officially covered in the appetizer department.

Oysters with All the Sauces

Back in my picky-eating days, you could not have paid me to eat an oyster. I convinced myself that they would be fishy, slimy, and all-around yuck. But what I discovered was that high-quality, fresh oysters are sweet and briny—almost like tasting the ocean. That's why when I serve them, I don't use overpowering condiments like horseradish or cocktail sauce. No, thank you! Instead, I offer a trio of mignonettes, or vinegar-based sauces, that bring out the natural flavor of the oysters.

Ingredients

For the classic mignonette:
½ cup (120 ml) red wine vinegar
2 tablespoons minced shallots
½ teaspoon freshly cracked black pepper

For the chive mignonette:
½ cup (120 ml) rice vinegar
1 tablespoon fresh lime juice
2 tablespoons chopped fresh chives
1 teaspoon sugar
½ teaspoon kosher salt

For the cucumber mignonette:
½ cup (120 ml) white wine vinegar
5 tablespoons (45 g) minced English cucumber
1 tablespoon minced shallot
1 tablespoon chopped fresh cilantro
½ teaspoon kosher salt

For the oysters:
24 oysters (I prefer smaller oysters like Kusshi)
Rock salt

To make each mignonette: Mix all the ingredients in a small bowl and chill for 30 minutes to let the flavors meld.

To prepare the oysters: Clean and shuck all the oysters. Set the rock salt on a large serving tray and lay the shucked oysters on top.

Stir each of the mignonettes and serve alongside the oysters. Enjoy immediately.

Serves 6 to 8 | Total Time: 40 minutes (Prep: 40. Cook: 0.)

Rainbow Summer Rolls

I would make these all the time when I was a private chef, especially when I was cooking for a crowd. They're nice and light, beyond simple to assemble, and add a super-colorful punch to the table. Feel free to get creative with this recipe—mix and match with your favorite veggies or even add cooked shrimp or crab if you want some extra protein.

Ingredients

For the dipping sauce:

¼ cup (60 ml) hoisin sauce
2 tablespoons smooth unsweetened peanut butter
1 teaspoon rice vinegar
2 teaspoons soy sauce, or to taste
1 teaspoon chili garlic sauce
½ teaspoon toasted sesame oil

For the summer rolls:

12 rice paper wrappers
1 cup (185 g) dry vermicelli rice noodles, cooked according to package directions
2 Persian cucumbers, thinly sliced
1 large carrot, thinly sliced
1 red bell pepper, thinly sliced
1 mango, pitted, peeled, and thinly sliced
3 scallions, white and light green parts, thinly sliced
½ cup (25 g) fresh mint leaves
½ cup (20 g) fresh basil leaves
½ cup (20 g) fresh cilantro leaves
2 ripe avocados, pitted, peeled, and thinly sliced
1 head butter lettuce

To make the dipping sauce: In a medium bowl, whisk together all the ingredients. Taste and add more soy sauce if you want it a bit saltier. Set aside until ready to serve.

To make the summer rolls: Fill a shallow bowl with water. Soak one rice paper wrapper in the water for 30 to 45 seconds, until pliable. Transfer the wrapper onto a clean cutting board. If it didn't get quite flexible enough to roll, briefly dip it in water again.

Arrange the fillings along the bottom third of the wrapper. I use about 2 tablespoons of the rice noodles; equal amounts of the cucumber, carrot, bell pepper, mango, and scallions; a few fresh mint, basil, and cilantro leaves; 2 avocado slices; and a butter lettuce leaf for each roll.

Fold the wrapper over the filling and start rolling it up. About halfway through the roll, stop and fold in the sides, burrito style. Then finish rolling until you have a tight roll. Transfer the finished roll to a clean plate seam side down and drape with a damp kitchen towel while you assemble and roll the remaining summer rolls. Once all of the rolls are finished, serve immediately with the dipping sauce alongside.

Serves 4 to 6 | Total Time: 15 minutes (Prep: 15. Cook: 0.)

Matt's Bean *and* Cheese Panchos

When your best friend (and food photographer) says you need panchos in your cookbook, you listen. These are basically single-serving nachos, or crispy corn tortillas, that are loaded up with beans, cheese, and of course, guacamole. It's a fun twist on the Tex-Mex food staple—especially because you don't have to share!

Ingredients

¼ cup (60 ml) vegetable oil
6 corn tortillas, cut in half
1 cup (115 g) shredded cheddar cheese
1 cup (115 g) shredded pepper Jack cheese
1½ cups (255 g) refried pinto beans, warmed
4½ ounces (130 g) Mexican chorizo, cooked and drained
½ cup (120 ml) sour cream
½ teaspoon ground cumin
½ teaspoon ground coriander
Juice of 1 lime
Kosher salt and freshly ground black pepper
½ cup (50 g) pickled jalapeño chiles
4 ounces (115 g) cotija cheese, crumbled
½ cup (20 g) chopped fresh cilantro
2 scallions, white and light green parts, chopped
Gaby's Famous Guacamole (page 27)

Preheat the oven to 375°F (190°C). Line two baking sheets with parchment paper or aluminum foil.

In a large skillet, heat the oil over medium-high heat. Add a few tortilla halves to the oil and fry until crispy on both sides, 2 to 3 minutes total, turning halfway through. Remove to a paper towel–lined plate to cool slightly and let excess oil drip off. Repeat until you've fried all of the tortilla halves.

In a medium bowl, combine the cheddar and Jack cheeses and set aside.

Place the fried tostada halves on the prepared baking sheets. Working assembly-line style, place about 2 tablespoons of warmed refried beans on each tostada half, sprinkle on the cheese mixture, and top with the chorizo.

Bake for 8 to 10 minutes, until the cheese is melted.

While the panchos are in the oven, in a medium bowl, whisk together the sour cream, cumin, coriander, and lime juice. Season with salt and pepper.

Remove the panchos from the oven, top with the pickled jalapeños, a drizzle of spiced sour cream, the cotija cheese, cilantro, and scallions, and serve with the guacamole.

Serves 6 | Total Time: 25 minutes (Prep: 15. Cook: 10.)

California Girl Cheese Board

Ingredients

Humboldt Fog goat cheese
Monterey Jack or pepper Jack cheese
Red Hawk cheese
Gouda cheese
Burrata cheese
Fiscalini Bandaged Cheddar cheese
Thinly sliced prosciutto
Thinly sliced salami
Marcona almonds
Pistachios
Candied walnuts
Olives
Crackers
Breadsticks
Dried fruit
Fresh fruit
Dried Strawberry and Cherry Compote (recipe below)

There's not much more to putting together the perfect cheese board than loading up as many goodies on there as possible and making them look pretty. But there are a few good rules of thumb. Make sure to get a range of cheeses: soft, hard, mild, intense, cow, goat. I like seeking out California-made options, and I encourage you to see what kinds of cheeses are being made near you. Pair them with lots of different crackers and breadsticks for variety, along with other salty or sweet nibbles like olives (a must), salumi, nuts, fresh or dried fruit, and compote (wait until you try the compote: GAME CHANGER. Plus it can be made weeks in advance).

Let the cheeses sit at room temperature for about thirty minutes before serving and cut a few slices from each piece to not only make them look more appealing, but also to help your guests feel less shy about being the first ones to dig in. Although if you're inviting me over, I have no issue being the first one to dig into a cheese platter! No shame in my game.

Serves 8+ | Total Time: 10 minutes (Prep: 10. Cook: 0.)

Dried Strawberry + Cherry Compote

4 ounces (115 g) dried strawberries, roughly chopped
4 ounces (115 g) dried cherries, roughly chopped
2 cups (480 ml) water
¼ cup (60 ml) fresh orange juice
1 tablespoon fresh lemon juice
⅓ cup (65 g) sugar
½ cinnamon stick
1 whole clove
1 star anise pod
Pinch of kosher salt

In a medium saucepan, combine the dried fruit and water. Place over medium-high heat, bring to a simmer, reduce heat to medium, and simmer for 15 minutes, or until the fruit is soft but still keeps its shape. Add the orange juice, lemon juice, sugar, cinnamon, clove, star anise, and salt, and continue cooking until the liquid has reduced to a syrupy consistency, about 8 more minutes. Remove from heat and let cool to room temperature before serving. The compote can be made ahead of time and stored in the refrigerator in an airtight container for up to 3 weeks.

Pea Pesto *and* Burrata Crostini

Traditionally, pesto is a blend of basil, Parmesan, and pine nuts. But you can turn just about anything into a pesto, so long as there's a fresh element, whether it's an herb or a vegetable. When spring rolls around and peas are out in full force, I'm all about a pesto that features peas. Their naturally sweet flavor paired with basil, mint, and garlic along with a decadent soft cheese like burrata makes for the perfect crostini topper. If you can't find burrata, then you should just move . . . joking! Fresh mozzarella works, too.

Ingredients

For the pea pesto:

1 (10-ounce/280-g) package frozen peas, thawed, or 10 ounces (280 g) fresh peas, blanched and cooled
⅓ cup (15 g) fresh basil leaves
⅓ cup (17 g) fresh mint leaves
1 clove garlic, peeled
Juice of 1 lemon
½ teaspoon red pepper flakes
Kosher salt and freshly cracked black pepper

For the crostini:

1 baguette, cut into ½-inch (12-mm) slices
Olive oil
2 cloves garlic, peeled

For assembly:

6 ounces burrata cheese
Pea tendrils, or extra basil and/or mint

To make the pesto: In a large food processor, combine the peas, basil, mint, garlic, lemon juice, and red pepper flakes and season with salt and pepper. Pulse for 45 seconds, until the peas are broken down and chunky. Scrape down the sides of the bowl and pulse for an additional 10 seconds. Taste and adjust the salt and pepper as needed.

To make the crostini: Heat a griddle or large skillet over medium-high heat.

Generously drizzle the baguette slices with oil on both sides. Using tongs, transfer the slices of bread to the hot griddle and toast for a few moments, until golden brown. Flip and toast the bread on the other side for a minute more. Remove from the griddle and set aside. Carefully rub the garlic over the toasted bread.

To assemble: Slather 2 tablespoons of the pea pesto on top of each crostini. Add a tablespoon or two of burrata cheese and garnish with some pea tendrils. Serve immediately.

Serves 6 to 8 | Total Time: 10 minutes (Prep: 5. Cook: 5.)

Extra pea pesto can be tossed into pasta for a quick and easy weeknight dinner.

Bruschetta Bar

If I had a signature spread for entertaining, this would be it. It's my favorite way to feed a crowd because everyone can assemble their own bites. And because there's so much to choose from—Meats! Cheeses! Sautéed veggies! Sauces! Dips!—there's bound to be something that every guest will want to eat. Yes, there are a lot of elements here, but every single one can be used in other ways, such as tossed in salads, slathered on sandwiches, or heaped into rice bowls. For a more polished occasion, you can assemble and style the bruschetta bar yourself, or for a casual picnic or potluck, assign guests something to bring.

Ingredients

1 large loaf of bread, cut into ½-inch (12-mm) slices
2 tablespoons olive oil, plus more for brushing the bread
2 cloves garlic, peeled
2 yellow onions, thinly sliced
Basil Vinaigrette (page 250)
Saffron Tomato Confit (page 264)
Romesco Sauce (page 32)
Green Goddess Dip (page 260)
Spring Pea Pesto (page 20)
Handful of fresh arugula
½ cup (65 g) Garlic Wild Mushrooms (page 116)
Assorted cheeses such as burrata, ricotta, and goat cheese
Assorted meats such as salami and prosciutto

Heat a griddle or large skillet over medium-high heat.

Generously drizzle the bread with oil on both sides. Using tongs, transfer the bread slices to the griddle and toast for a few moments, until golden brown. Flip and toast the bread on the other side for a minute more. Remove from the griddle. Carefully rub the garlic over the toasted bread.

To make the caramelized onions, heat a large, heavy skillet over medium heat and add remaining 2 tablespoons oil. Add the onions and stir to combine. Once the onions start to cook down, reduce heat to medium low and continue to cook, stirring occasionally, until golden and caramelized, about 25 minutes.

Arrange the toppings on a large platter and serve with the grilled bread. Let guests DIY their own bruschetta toppings.

Serves 8+ | Total Time: 35 minutes (Prep: 10. Cook: 25.)

Pepper Jack Bean Dip

I feel very strongly about a good bean dip because, Hi, I grew up in Arizona. Any Southwestern girl will tell you that the keys to this game-day staple are cheese and spice, so using pepper Jack cheese is one way to nail both, plus green chiles, cumin, and chili powder for extra kick. I'd tell you that leftovers would be awesome slathered on a quesadilla or served over rice with a spoonful of salsa or guacamole—but I've never actually had leftovers.

Ingredients

2 teaspoons olive oil
1 yellow onion, finely diced
4 cloves garlic, roughly chopped
1 teaspoon ground cumin
1 teaspoon chili powder
1 teaspoon kosher salt
½ teaspoon red pepper flakes
2 (16-ounce/455-g) cans refried pinto beans
1 (14.5-ounce/415-g) can diced tomatoes, juices drained
1 (4-ounce/115-g) can diced green chiles
⅓ cup (75 ml) sour cream
2 cups (230 g) shredded pepper Jack cheese
Juice of 1 lime
4 scallions, white and light green parts, thinly sliced
2 tablespoons chopped fresh cilantro
Tortilla chips

Preheat the broiler.

In an oven-safe skillet, heat the oil over medium-high heat. Add the onion and cook for 3 to 4 minutes, until translucent. Add the garlic, cumin, chili powder, salt, and red pepper flakes and cook for 1 minute, or until fragrant. Add the refried beans and stir until warmed through.

Remove from the heat and add the drained diced tomatoes, green chiles, sour cream, 1 cup (115 g) of the cheese, and the lime juice. Stir until fully combined, then press the mixture in an even layer. Top with the remaining 1 cup (115 g) cheese. Place under the broiler and broil for 3 to 4 minutes, until the cheese is golden brown.

Remove from the oven and garnish with the scallions and cilantro. Serve immediately with tortilla chips for dipping.

Serves 8 | Total Time: 15 minutes (Prep: 5. Cook: 10.)

Gaby's Famous Guacamole

Leave it to me to write an entire cookbook on avocados and only discover the secret to the best guac in the world after I finish! But here it is: no chopped tomatoes, mayo, garlic, or any of the other weird things people are putting in it these days. (Broccoli and peas? No thank you.) Just avocados and a few ingredients to help balance their creamy richness, like lemon, lime, chives, and jalapeños. Simple and perfect.

Ingredients

4 ripe avocados, pitted, flesh scooped out, peels discarded
Juice of 1 lemon, or to taste
Juice of 1 lime, or to taste
Kosher salt and freshly cracked black pepper
⅓ cup (35 g) finely chopped red onion
3 to 4 tablespoons chopped fresh chives
2 teaspoons finely chopped jalapeño chile
Tortilla chips

Put the avocado flesh in a large bowl. Add the lemon juice and lime juice and season with salt and pepper. Mash with a fork until smooth and creamy. Stir in the red onion, chives, and jalapeño. Taste and adjust the lemon juice, lime juice, salt, and pepper if needed.

Serve immediately with tortilla chips for scooping.

Serves 4 to 6 | Total Time: 5 minutes (Prep: 5. Cook: 0.)

California Girl Margarita

1 wedge of lime
Kosher salt
5 ounces (150 ml) tequila
5 ounces (150 ml) freshly squeezed citrus juice—orange, blood orange, tangerine, satsuma, or grapefruit
3 ounces (90 ml) lime juice
2 teaspoons agave nectar
Splash of sparkling water

Run a wedge of lime across the top of 2 cocktail glasses. Once damp, coat the rims in salt. Add all the ingredients except the sparkling water into a cocktail shaker with a few cubes of ice. Shake for 30 seconds, until chilled, and then strain the margaritas into serving glasses with new ice. Top each glass with a splash of sparkling water and serve immediately.

Citrus-Marinated Olives

I loved olives as a kid. Every night before dinner I'd put a big black olive on each finger and eat them one by one. But believe it or not, I kinda OD'd on olives. It wasn't until recently that I fell in love again, just in time for my birthday trip to Italy last year, where I ate any olive in arm's reach. (It also helps that my husband doesn't like olives—more for me!) My favorite is almost-neon green castelvetranos, or what I like to call "gateway olives," because they're so mild in flavor. They're pretty perfect on their own, but marinating them with lots of citrus, garlic, and herbs gives them an extra-special twist.

Ingredients

¼ cup (60 ml) extra-virgin olive oil
3 cloves garlic, peeled
1 shallot, sliced
4 to 5 thyme sprigs
½ teaspoon red pepper flakes
2 cups (310 g) castelvetrano olives
½ lemon, zested into thick strips

In a small saucepan, combine the oil, garlic, shallot, thyme, and red pepper flakes. Place over medium heat and cook until the garlic starts to sizzle, 1 to 2 minutes, then reduce the heat to low and continue to cook for 10 minutes, until the oil is infused with garlic. Remove the pan from the heat and let steep for 1 hour.

Meanwhile, place the olives in a medium bowl and add the strips of lemon zest. Pour the oil mixture over the olives and stir to coat. Marinate at room temperature for 3 to 4 hours so the flavors can combine, or cover and chill for up to 4 days. Bring to room temperature before serving.

Serves 4 to 6 | Total Time: 4 to 5 hours (Prep: 3. Cook: 12.)

Poblano-Scallion Queso

Similar to my feelings on bean dip, queso—or gooey cheese that's been dressed up with all kinds of goodness like charred poblano peppers and peppery scallions—is mandatory for all sporting-related events at my house. This spicy, smoky version also showcases one of my favorite cheeses, Oaxaca, which is mild like mozzarella, has a string cheese–like texture, and melts like a dream. Pair this master creation with freshly made tortilla chips. And guacamole. And maybe a margarita, too (page 27). The only requirement is that you serve it ASAP for maximum cheese pull.

Ingredients

2 poblano peppers
2 tablespoons unsalted butter
1 yellow onion, finely chopped
3 scallions, white and light green parts, thinly sliced
1 cup (115 g) shredded Monterey Jack cheese
1 cup (115 g) shredded Oaxaca cheese
2 cups (230 g) shredded pepper Jack cheese
2 tablespoons milk
Chopped fresh cilantro
Tortilla chips

Preheat the broiler.

Place the poblano peppers on a baking sheet and place directly under the broiler. Broil, turning a few times with tongs, until blackened on all sides, 6 to 8 minutes total. Remove from the broiler and place in a bowl, covering it with plastic wrap to steam. After steaming for 15 to 20 minutes, the peppers will be cool enough to handle, then remove the skin, chop the flesh, and set aside. Alternatively, you can char the poblano peppers over an open flame on the stove, turning with tongs until all sides are charred, before steaming.

Adjust the oven temperature to 425°F (220°C).

In a 2-inch-deep (5-cm-deep) cast-iron skillet, melt the butter over medium-high heat. Add the onion, scallions, and roasted peppers and cook until the onion is softened, about 5 minutes. Top the onion and pepper mixture with the cheeses. Add the milk and stir to combine.

Pour hot water to come 1 inch (2.5 cm) up the sides of a roasting pan or baking dish. The baking dish must be big enough to accomodate the skillet. Place the skillet inside the water bath, making sure the water doesn't come close enough to spill into the skillet, and transfer to the oven. Bake until the cheese is melted and gooey, 20 to 25 minutes. Remove from the oven, sprinkle with cilantro, and serve immediately with tortilla chips.

Serves 8 | Total Time: 65 minutes (Prep: 5. Cook: 60.)

California Crudités

Romesco Sauce

Romesco sauce is like tomato sauce's smokier, spicier Spanish cousin, and I think it's something that should be made on a weekly basis. It works as a dip, a spread, a sauce, or just a tasty spoonful. While it's traditionally made with bread crumbs, I don't think you need them, and that also happens to make this recipe gluten-free. Just don't skimp on the smoked paprika—it's the star of the show.

2 roasted red bell peppers from a jar, drained
1 to 2 cloves garlic
¾ cup (100 g) unsalted almonds, cashews, or walnuts
1 tablespoon tomato paste
6 to 8 large fresh basil leaves
2 tablespoons red wine vinegar
½ teaspoon smoked paprika
½ teaspoon red pepper flakes
½ teaspoon kosher salt, or to taste
½ teaspoon freshly cracked black pepper, or to taste
¼ cup (60 ml) olive oil
Crackers, crostini, or crudités

Combine the roasted red peppers, garlic, almonds, tomato paste, basil, vinegar, paprika, red pepper flakes, salt, and pepper in a high-powered blender or food processor and blend for 1 minute, or until smooth. Stream in the olive oil while continuing to blend until completely smooth, another 1 to 1½ minutes. Taste and adjust the salt and pepper as needed. Serve with crackers, crostini, or crudités.

Serves 6 | Total Time: 5 minutes (Prep: 5. Cook: 0.)

Cucumber Dill Tzatziki

1½ cups (360 ml) plain 2% Greek yogurt
1 Persian cucumber, finely chopped (⅓ to ½ cup/35 to 50 g)
3 tablespoons fresh lemon juice, or to taste
3 cloves garlic, minced
3 tablespoon chopped fresh dill
1 teaspoon kosher salt, or to taste
½ teaspoon freshly cracked black pepper, or to taste

In a large bowl, combine the yogurt, cucumber, lemon juice, garlic, dill, salt, and pepper and stir to incorporate the ingredients. Taste and adjust the salt, pepper, or lemon juice if needed. Serve immediately or store in an airtight container in the refrigerator for up to 3 days.

Serves 6 | Total Time: 5 minutes (Prep: 5. Cook: 0.)

Lemon and Garlic Hummus

My addiction to hummus is real. I can go through a cup of it in a day, no problem. It stands to reason that I'm very serious about making the best version possible—and doing anything it takes to get there. So hear me out when I say that the secret to the creamiest, smoothest hummus ever is . . . peeling the chickpeas. I know it's annoying, but trust me, the result is totally worth it. Just lay them out on a clean, flat surface and either snap the skin off with your thumb and pointer finger, or place them on a clean dish towel, fold the towel over, and rub the chickpeas in the towel to start peeling off the skin. Then finish peeling them by hand.

1 (15-ounce/430-g) can chickpeas, drained, rinsed, and peeled
½ cup (120 ml) tahini
¼ cup (60 ml) fresh lemon juice, plus more if needed
2 cloves garlic, or to taste, peeled
1 teaspoon kosher salt, or to taste
4 to 6 tablespoons (60 to 90 ml) water
Extra-virgin olive oil
Dried sumac

In a food processor, process the chickpeas by themselves for 1 minute, or until powdery clumps form. Scrape down the sides and process again for 30 seconds.

Add the tahini, lemon juice, garlic, and salt and process until smooth. With the machine running, drizzle in 1 tablespoon of water at a time through the hole in the lid until you get a very smooth, light, and creamy mixture. Taste and adjust the seasonings, adding more salt, garlic, or lemon juice if needed.

Transfer to a serving bowl, drizzle with a little oil, sprinkle with sumac, and serve.

Serves 6 | Total Time: 5 minutes (Prep: 5. Cook: 0.)

Artichoke + Smoked Paprika Hummus

1 (15-ounce/430-g) can chickpeas, drained, rinsed, and peeled
1 (14-ounce/400-g)) can artichoke hearts packed in water, drained
½ cup (120 ml) tahini
3 tablespoons fresh lemon juice, or to taste
2 cloves garlic, or to taste, peeled
2 teaspoons smoked paprika, plus more for dusting
1 teaspoon kosher salt, or to taste
3 tablespoons water
Extra-virgin olive oil

In a food processor, process the chickpeas by themselves for 1 minute, or until clumps form. Scrape down the sides and process again for 30 seconds. Add the artichoke hearts, tahini, lemon juice, garlic, smoked paprika, and salt and process until smooth. With the machine running, drizzle in 1 tablespoon of water at a time through the hole in the lid until you get a very smooth, light, and creamy mixture. Taste and adjust the seasonings, adding more salt, garlic, or lemon juice if needed. Transfer to a serving bowl, drizzle with a little olive oil, sprinkle with smoked paprika, and serve.

Serves 6 | Total Time: 5 minutes (Prep: 5. Cook: 0.)

Chapter 2:

Breakfast + Brunch

If breakfast is the most important meal of the day—and it sure is in my book—then brunch is the most important meal of the WEEK. There's nothing like gathering a bunch of friends on the weekend for a yummy spread and eating the day away. Whether you're a fan of sweet, savory, or both, this chapter has what you're craving, from avocado toasts that change with the seasons to monkey bread that's so good you might not want to make it if you're home alone.

Breakfast Flatbread *with* Ricotta *and* Strawberry-Basil Jam

I've been obsessed with the strawberry-basil combo ever since making Strawberry-Basil Lemonade for my blog a few years back. It was the first recipe of mine to go viral, and I think it's because it's genius! The basil gives the sweet fruitiness of the berries a sophisticated note that's still fresh and fun. The sweet-savory mash-up is perfect for a jam, and even more perfect for topping a pizza with homemade ricotta for a showstopping brunch. You'll notice that the jam recipe makes about 2 cups (480 ml), but you only need 1 cup (240 ml) for this flatbread. Stash the extra in the fridge; or use it as a filling for doughnuts!

Ingredients

For the ricotta cheese:

2 quarts (2 L) whole milk
1 cup (240 ml) heavy cream
½ cup (120 ml) plain 2% Greek yogurt
1½ teaspoons fresh lemon juice
1½ teaspoons white vinegar
1 teaspoon Maldon sea salt

For the strawberry-basil jam:

1 quart (580 g) fresh strawberries, hulled and halved
⅓ cup (65 g) sugar
1 tablespoon fresh lemon juice
Pinch of kosher salt
4 fresh basil leaves

For the flatbread:

1 pound (455 g) store-bought pizza dough, divided into 4 equal pieces
All-purpose flour, for rolling
3 tablespoons honey
Maldon sea salt
Freshly cracked black pepper

To make the ricotta cheese: Line a colander with 4 to 5 layers of cheesecloth. Make sure there is enough draping over the edges so it doesn't fall into the colander later in the process.

In a large, heavy-bottomed pot, combine the milk, cream, yogurt, lemon juice, vinegar, and salt. Bring to a simmer over medium heat and cook until the mixture begins to curdle with the curds separating from the whey. Pour the mixture into the lined colander and let drain for about 10 minutes, until all the liquid has drained off and the ricotta remains. Lift the cheesecloth up and transfer the ricotta to an airtight container, where it will keep, refrigerated, for up to 2 weeks.

To make the strawberry-basil jam: In a medium saucepan, combine the strawberries, sugar, lemon juice, and salt. Place over medium-high heat and cook, stirring often, until the strawberries are soft, bubbling, and syrupy, about 10 minutes. Toss in the basil, remove from the heat, and let cool. You can remove the basil before serving if you like, or keep it in. The jam can be made in advance; it will keep, stored in an airtight container in the refrigerator for up to a week.

(recipe continues)

To make the flatbread: Let the pizza dough rest at room temperature for 30 to 45 minutes before starting.

Preheat the oven to 450°F (230°C). Line two baking sheets with parchment paper.

On a lightly floured surface, roll or stretch each piece of dough into a rectangle (about 4 by 9 inches/10 by 23 cm), or as close as you can get. Place two pieces of dough on each prepared pan. Drizzle with the honey and sprinkle with salt and the pepper.

Bake for 8 to 12 minutes, until golden brown. If any bubbles rise up, you can pop them with a fork. Remove from the oven and let cool slightly.

To serve: Spread the ricotta over the flatbreads, leaving a ½-inch (12-mm) border. Top with heavy dollops of strawberry-basil jam and season with salt and pepper. Cut into 4 pieces each and serve.

Serves 4 | Total Time: 45 minutes (Prep: 15. Cook: 30.)

White Chocolate Macadamia Nut Cookie Scones

I have a lot of feelings about scones. They need to be big and fluffy and moist—probably more moist than a traditional scone is meant to be. I mean, if they're too dry, why even bother? Then I realized that the things I love in a scone are also the things I love in a cookie. So I took Thomas's favorite cookie—white chocolate–macadamia nut—and lent that to the ultimate scone recipe.

Ingredients

2½ cups (315 g) all-purpose flour
1 tablespoon baking powder
½ teaspoon kosher salt
¼ cup (55 g) brown sugar
5 tablespoons (75 g) cold unsalted butter, grated on the large holes of a box grater
1 cup (175 g) chopped white chocolate or white chocolate chips
½ cup plus 2 tablespoons (155 g) toasted macadamia nut pieces
1¼ cups (300 ml) heavy cream, plus more for brushing the scones
1 teaspoon vanilla extract
½ cup (85 g) white chocolate chunks or chips

Preheat the oven to 400°F (205°C). Line a baking sheet with parchment paper.

In a large bowl, combine the flour, baking powder, salt, and brown sugar and gently whisk together. Add the grated butter and toss to evenly distribute it. Fold in the chopped white chocolate and ½ cup (124 g) of the macadamia nut pieces. Make a well in the center and pour in the heavy cream and vanilla. Fold everything together just to incorporate; do not overwork the dough.

Turn the dough out onto a lightly floured surface. Shape into a rectangle about 12 inches (30 cm) long and 3 inches (8 cm) wide. Cut the log into 5 equal squares, then cut them diagonally to create 10 triangles. Arrange them on the prepared baking sheet and brush the tops with heavy cream.

Bake for 16 to 20 minutes, until the tops just barely turn golden brown. Remove from the oven and place the scones on a wire rack set over a piece of parchment paper.

While the scones are cooling, melt the white chocolate in a microwave-safe bowl on high for 30 seconds, stir, and then continue to microwave in 10-second intervals until melted. Pour the melted white chocolate into a zip-top bag and snip off a small corner. Drizzle the melted white chocolate over the scones, quickly sprinkle with the remaining 2 tablespoons macadamia nut pieces, and serve, or, once the chocolate has cooled, store in an airtight container for up to 1 week.

Serves 10 | Total Time: 25 minutes (Prep: 5. Cook: 20.)

Thomas's Perfect California Breakfast Burrito

Breakfast burritos are serious business in our household. Growing up in Arizona, these eggy, spicy, bacon-y roll-ups were a staple. Then Thomas took them to the next level when he and some friends at work started Club Rito. Every Friday, someone would bring burritos for the group, and they'd grade them on a number of criteria: Are the eggs perfectly scrambled? Is the bacon evenly distributed? Are all the ingredients in an ideal ratio? So I can tell you with almost scientific certainty that this recipe makes perfect breakfast burritos.

Ingredients

4 strips bacon (or cooked chorizo or sausage)
8 large eggs
1 tablespoon unsalted butter or olive oil
Kosher salt and freshly cracked black pepper
4 large flour tortillas
1 cup (115 g) grated cheddar cheese
1 cup (165 g) Pico de Gallo (recipe below)
2 cups (280 g) Perfect Roasted Potatoes (page 115)
2 ripe avocados, pitted, peeled, and sliced
Chipotle salsa

Cook the bacon in a large cast-iron skillet over medium-high heat until crispy on both sides. Remove from the skillet to a plate to cool, then crumble into small pieces.

Crack the eggs into a bowl and whisk until smooth.

In a large skillet, melt the butter over medium heat. Add the eggs and softly scramble them. Season with salt and pepper.

Warm each tortilla over an open flame to make them as pliable as possible. Alternatively, if you have an electric stove, warm the tortillas in a microwave in 30-second bursts until warmed through. To assemble, lay the tortillas on a clean, flat surface. Divide the cooked eggs equally over each tortilla in a line, followed by the bacon, cheese, pico de gallo, roasted potatoes, and sliced avocado (it's important that everything is evenly distributed so when you roll them up you get all the flavors in each bite).

Fold the ends of the tortillas in and roll the burritos up. Serve immediately with the salsa alongside.

Serves 4 | Total Time: 20 minutes (Prep: 10. Cook: 10.)

Pico de Gallo

1½ pounds (680 g) ripe tomatoes, cut into ¼- to ½-inch (6- to 12-mm) dice
½ large white onion, finely diced (about ¾ cup/95 g)
1 to 2 jalapeño chiles, finely diced (seeds and membranes removed for a milder salsa)
½ cup (20 g) finely chopped cilantro leaves
1 tablespoon fresh lime juice
Kosher salt

In a large bowl combine the tomatoes, onion, jalapeño, cilantro, and lime juice. Gently toss to combine. Season with salt to taste.

Dad's Pepper Jack, Bacon, and Corona Beer Bread

My dad is a self-taught master baker. Seriously, he does it all—breads, cookies, muffins. There's never been a time when I've gone home to visit and the house hasn't been stocked with freshly baked goods. This beer bread is one of my favorites, and it couldn't be easier to make. I've jazzed things up with pepper Jack cheese, bacon, and scallions, and I use Corona for a beach-y twist. Serve this bread warm, slathered with butter and a sprinkling of Maldon sea salt.

Ingredients

Nonstick cooking spray
3 cups (375 g) all-purpose flour
3 tablespoons sugar
4½ teaspoons baking powder
½ teaspoon kosher salt
½ teaspoon freshly cracked black pepper
1½ cups (360 ml) Corona (or another Mexican beer)
1 cup (115 g) shredded pepper Jack cheese
5 strips cooked bacon, crumbled into tiny pieces
2 scallions, white and light green parts, ends trimmed and thinly sliced
Unsalted butter, at room temperature
Maldon sea salt

Preheat the oven to 375°F (190°C). Spray a 9 by 5-inch (23 by 13-cm) loaf pan with cooking spray.

In a large bowl, combine the flour, sugar, baking powder, kosher salt, and pepper and whisk to combine. Add the beer and stir until evenly incorporated. Fold in the cheese, bacon, and scallions until evenly combined. Transfer the dough to the prepared baking pan and place in the oven.

Bake for 55 minutes, or until the top is golden brown. Remove from the oven, cut into ½- to ¾-inch (12- to 20-mm) slices, slather with butter, and sprinkle with Maldon sea salt. Serve warm.

Serves 6 to 8 | Total Time: 1 hour and 5 minutes (Prep: 10. Cook: 55.)

Smoothies
for All Seasons

Between living in LA and being walking distance to about 12,398 smoothie bars—and having a best friend who is obsessed with smoothies (I'm looking at you, Catherine)—I couldn't include just one smoothie recipe. After all, my smoothie tastes change with my mood and time of year. You can mix it up with tropical fruits (my ode to Orange Julius); fresh farmers' market produce; cacao powder and dates (if you're feeling a little naughty); or blueberries and bananas (my personal favorite). ***Pro tip:*** *It pays to get the best coconut water possible—the kind that's never been pasteurized. Splurge on the good stuff, and your smoothie game will be next level.*

Banana–Mango–Orange Julius Smoothie *(Spring)*

1 cup (165 g) frozen mango, diced
1 ripe banana, sliced
1 cup (240 ml) fresh orange juice
1 teaspoon chia seeds
3 to 5 ice cubes

Combine all the ingredients in a high-powered blender and blend for 1 to 2 minutes, until completely smooth and the chia seeds are finely ground. Pour into glasses and serve.

Serves 2 | Total Time: 2 minutes (Prep: 2. Cook: 0.)

Strawberry, Pineapple, and Coconut Smoothie *(Summer)*

2 cups (300 g) frozen strawberries, sliced
1 cup (165 g) frozen pineapple, diced
1 ripe banana, sliced
1¼ cups (300 ml) fresh coconut water

Combine all the ingredients in a high-powered blender and blend for 1 to 2 minutes, until completely smooth. Pour into glasses and serve.

Serves 2 | Total Time: 2 minutes (Prep: 2. Cook: 0.)

Blueberry Bliss Smoothie *(Fall)*

1 cup (155 g) frozen blueberries
1 ripe banana, sliced
2 tablespoons almond butter
1 cup (240 ml) vanilla almond milk
1 scoop vanilla plant-based protein powder (optional)

Combine all the ingredients in a high-powered blender and blend for 1 to 2 minutes, until completely smooth. Pour into glasses and serve.

Serves 2 | Total Time: 2 minutes (Prep: 2. Cook: 0.)

Chocolate, Cashew, and Date Smoothie *(Winter)*

1 or 2 Medjool dates, pitted
1 ripe banana, sliced
1 tablespoon cacao powder
1 cup (240 ml) cashew milk
2 tablespoons cashew butter
⅛ teaspoon ground cinnamon
¼ teaspoon vanilla extract
Handful of ice cubes

Combine all the ingredients except the ice in a high-powered blender and blend for 1 to 2 minutes, until completely smooth. Add the ice and blend again until smooth. Pour into glasses and serve.

Serves 2 | Total Time: 2 minutes (Prep: 2. Cook: 0.)

Caramelized Onion, Leek, *and* Red Pepper Crustless Quiche

I've always wanted to be one of those people who could whip up brunch for friends at a moment's notice, including a perfectly flaky crust for a quiche. But I'm mature enough to know that I'm just not that kind of girl. A crustless quiche, on the other hand—that I can do, no sweat. No one will miss the crust with this delicious version loaded up with caramelized onions, mushrooms, and Fontina cheese, so now you can totally be that person who hosts a leisurely, effortless Sunday brunch.

Ingredients

Nonstick cooking spray
3 tablespoons panko bread crumbs
2 tablespoons olive oil
1 onion, thinly sliced
3 leeks, white and light green parts, cleaned, trimmed, and cut into ½-inch (12-mm) slices
7 ounces (200 g) fresh shiitake mushrooms, stems removed, thinly sliced
1 red bell pepper, thinly sliced
Kosher salt and freshly cracked black pepper
1 cup (110 g) shredded Fontina cheese
4 large eggs
1 cup (240 ml) heavy cream
1 cup (240 ml) whole milk
Market greens tossed with olive oil and lemon juice (optional)

Preheat the oven to 425°F (220°C). Spray a quiche pan (9 inches wide and 2 inches deep/23 cm wide and 5 cm deep) with nonstick cooking spray, then sprinkle the panko all over.

Heat a large, heavy skillet over medium heat and add the oil. Add the onion, leeks, and mushrooms and cook, stirring occasionally, until caramelized, about 25 minutes. Add the red pepper and cook for about 5 minutes more, until softened. Season with salt and pepper, transfer the vegetable mixture into the quiche pan, and sprinkle the cheese evenly over the top.

In a large bowl, whisk together the eggs, cream, milk, ½ teaspoon salt, and ¼ teaspoon pepper and pour the mixture over the cheese.

Bake until the top is golden and the custard is set in the center, 25 to 30 minutes. Cool slightly, then cut into wedges and serve, with dressed market greens if you like.

Serves 6 to 8 | Total Time: 1 hour and 10 minutes
(Prep: 10. Cook: 1 hour.)

RUMFORD
THE WHOLESOME BAKING POWDER

Cinnamon Roll-Chocolate Chip Monkey Bread

OMG BE WARNED: This is dangerous. It's a combination of cinnamon rolls, monkey bread, and chocolate chip cookies. The sugars get caramelized, toffee-like, and gooey, and the chocolate chips are perfectly melted. It's hands-down the best sweet breakfast to ever come out of my kitchen, so unless you want to eat it all yourself, invite people over to share it with you.

Ingredients

For the monkey bread:

1⅓ cups (315 ml) warm water (about 110°F/43°C)
½ cup (1 stick/115 g) plus 2 tablespoons unsalted butter, melted, plus softened butter for greasing the bowl
¼ cup (65 g) granulated sugar
1 (.25-ounce/7-g) package instant yeast
3¼ cups (405 g) all-purpose flour, plus extra for the work surface
2 teaspoons kosher salt
1 cup (220 g) light brown sugar
2 teaspoons ground cinnamon
1 cup (185 g) mini chocolate chips

For the glaze:

1 cup (125 g) powdered sugar
2 tablespoons almond milk
½ teaspoon vanilla extract

To make the monkey bread: In a large bowl, combine the warm water, 2 tablespoons of the melted butter, the granulated sugar, and yeast and let sit for 5 minutes. Combine the flour and salt in a stand mixer fitted with the dough hook. Turn the machine to low and slowly add the liquid mixture to the flour mixture until the dough comes together, then increase the speed to medium and mix until the dough is shiny and smooth, 6 to 7 minutes. Turn the dough onto a lightly floured counter and knead briefly to form a smooth, round ball. Grease a large bowl with butter and place the dough in the bowl. Cover the bowl with plastic wrap and place in a warm area until it doubles in size, 50 to 60 minutes.

While the dough is rising, in a small bowl, combine the brown sugar, cinnamon, and mini chocolate chips. Pour the remaining ½ cup (115 g) melted butter into a second bowl and set aside.

Gently remove the dough from the bowl and pat it into a rough 8-inch (20-cm) square. Using a bench scraper or knife, cut the dough into 64 pieces. Roll each piece of dough into a ball. One at a time, dip the balls into the melted butter. Roll in the brown sugar mixture, then layer the balls in a 9-inch (23-cm) round baking pan in 2 or 3 layers. Let the unbaked dough rest, uncovered, for another 45 minutes.

Preheat the oven to 350°F (175°C). Place the pan in the oven and bake until the top is deep brown and caramel begins to bubble around the edges, about 35 minutes. Cool the bread in the pan for 5 minutes, then turn out onto a platter and cool for about 10 minutes.

To make the glaze: Whisk ingredients in a small bowl and drizzle the glaze over the bread. Serve warm.

Serves 6 to 8 | Total Time: About 2 hours (Prep: 20. Cook: 35.)

Chocolate-Studded Banana Bread Muffins

Working as a private chef for a family taught me how handy it is to make large batches of muffins and pack them up in the freezer so they're ready to grab and reheat for breakfast, an addition to a school lunch or an afternoon snack. Chocolate and bananas are a match made in muffin heaven—or loaf heaven, if you decide to make this recipe in a loaf pan instead. Just bake a bit longer, about 55 minutes in a 9 by 5-inch (23 by 13-cm) loaf pan.

Ingredients

Nonstick cooking spray
¾ cup (1½ sticks/170 g) unsalted butter, at room temperature
1½ cups (300 g) sugar
2 large eggs
2 tablespoons almond milk
4 overripe bananas (as speckled black on the skin as possible)
2 cups (250 g) all-purpose flour
1 teaspoon baking soda
1 cup (175 g) dark chocolate chips

Preheat the oven to 350°F (175°C). Spray two 12-cup muffin pans with cooking spray.

In a stand mixer, mix the butter and sugar for 2 minutes, or until combined. Add the eggs one at a time, scraping down the sides of the bowl to evenly incorporate the ingredients. Add the almond milk and bananas and mix for 30 seconds. The batter will look a little curdled—this is normal. Add the flour and baking soda and mix for a few seconds, until the flour is evenly combined. Add the chocolate chips and give it a quick stir.

Evenly divide the batter among the muffin cups, using about ¼ cup (60 ml) batter per muffin cup. Bake for 27 to 30 minutes, until the muffins are fully baked and the tops spring back when touched. If you insert a toothpick into the center of the muffin, it should come out clean. Remove the muffins from the pans to a wire rack and let cool for at least 15 minutes before serving.

Serves 12 (makes 2 dozen) | Total Time: 35 minutes (Prep: 5. Cook: 30.)

Chocolate-Coconut Granola

I'm the kind of person who really likes to snack. I'm talking about a handful of something fabulous every half hour—seriously. I keep telling myself it's because I get grumpy if I don't eat, but really . . . I just like snacking! There's nothing wrong with that, right? Granola is something I'm always sure to have on hand, whether it's to spoon over yogurt in the morning, grab for a last-minute weekend trip, or to quench my serious all-day munching addiction (especially before dinner, instead of reaching for chips and salsa—yet again). This is one of my favorite (mostly healthy) versions—the coconut makes the whole mix feel tropical and sunny, while the chocolate chips are a little naughty. I love that you can go crazy with all kinds of different ingredients here—change up the dried fruit or nuts, or swap out chocolate for butterscotch chips, go crazy! Go with whatever you're in the mood for or whatever's in your pantry.

Ingredients

3 cups (270 g) old-fashioned oats
¾ cup (100 g) raw cashews, roughly chopped
¾ cup (105 g) almonds, roughly chopped
1 cup (85 g) unsweetened shredded coconut
1 teaspoon kosher salt
1 teaspoon ground cinnamon
½ cup (1 stick/115 g) unsalted butter
¼ cup (60 ml) agave nectar or honey
⅔ cup (145 g) packed brown sugar
2 teaspoons vanilla extract
½ cup (85 g) dark chocolate chips
½ cups (70 g) dried cranberries
½ cup (75 g) dried cherries
½ cup (65 g) dried apricots, chopped
Greek yogurt

Preheat the oven to 325°F (165°C). Line a large baking sheet with parchment paper.

In a large bowl, combine the oats, cashews, almonds, coconut, salt, and cinnamon. Set aside.

In a medium saucepan, combine the butter, agave, and brown sugar and cook over medium-low heat until the sugar has completely dissolved. Remove the pan from the heat and stir in the vanilla. Pour the butter mixture over the oat mixture and stir until everything is well coated.

Spread the granola mixture over the prepared baking sheet, leaving a few large clumps. Bake for 15 minutes, then remove from the oven and give the pan a good shake to ensure even baking. Bake for another 15 minutes, then remove the sheet from the oven and give it one more toss to break up some of the larger pieces. Bake for 10 more minutes; at this point the granola should be golden brown and a little crunchy. Let the granola cool completely on the pan, then add the chocolate chips and dried fruit. Give everything a quick toss with a spoon. Pack the granola in mason jars or airtight bags; it will keep for up to 2 weeks in the refrigerator. Serve with yogurt.

Serves 10 to 12 people (6 cups) | Total Time: 55 minutes (Prep: 10. Cook: 45.)

Avocado Toast
for All Seasons

Avocado toast is the ultimate meal on bread. All you need are avocados, good-quality bread, and whatever toppings you like—charred corn in the spring, grilled cheese-style in the summer, smoked salmon in fall, fried eggs and bacon for winter—just to name a few! Any way you do it up, it's such a great way to start the day. Avocados are pretty much the ideal food—nourishing and satisfying, yet so creamy and decadent. An avocado a day keeps the doctor away! Or at least that's what I like to think. I always have avocados in stock in my house, which means there will always be at least one that's ripe enough for avo toast.

Avocado Toast with Fresh Corn and Herbs (Spring)

2 (½-inch/12-mm) slices rustic bread (I love whole grain or use any seedy loaf from your favorite bakery)
1 ripe avocado, pitted, flesh scooped out, peel discarded
Kosher salt and freshly cracked black pepper
Juice of ½ lemon
⅓ cup (50 g) roasted corn kernels
2 tablespoons chopped fresh chives
A few fresh basil leaves

Toast the bread in a toaster or toaster oven. Smash the avocado in a medium bowl, season with salt and pepper, and add the lemon juice. Top each piece of toast with half of the avocado mixture. Sprinkle the top with roasted corn and season with salt and pepper. Top with the chives and basil and serve immediately.

Serves 2 | Total Time: 5 minutes (Prep: 5. Cook: 0.)

Avocado Halloumi Toast (Summer)

2 (½-inch/12-mm) slices rustic bread
1 ripe avocado, pitted, flesh scooped out, peel discarded
Kosher salt and freshly cracked black pepper
Juice of ½ lemon
1 teaspoon olive oil
4 ounces halloumi cheese, cut into ½-inch (12-mm) slices
1 heirloom tomato, cut into ½-inch (12-mm) slices

Toast the bread in a toaster or toaster oven. Smash the avocado in a medium bowl, season with salt and pepper, and add the lemon juice. Top each piece of toast with half of the avocado mixture.

Heat a nonstick skillet over medium-high heat and add the oil. Add the halloumi to the skillet and sear for about 2 minutes on each side, until golden brown. Remove from the skillet, evenly distribute the halloumi over the toast, and top with the sliced tomato. Season with salt and pepper and serve immediately.

Serves 2 | Total Time: 9 minutes (Prep: 5. Cook: 4.)

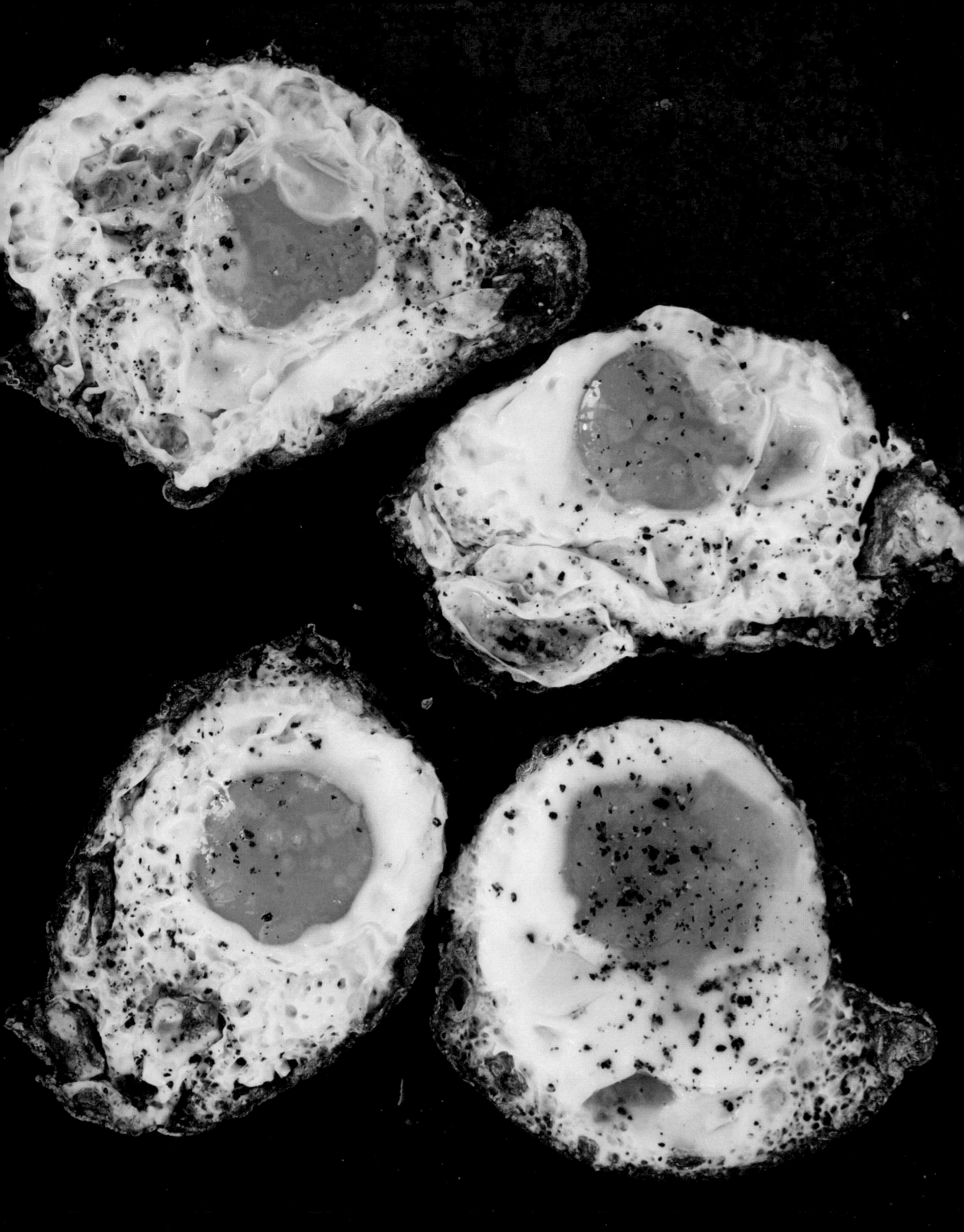

Avocado Toast with Smoked Salmon and Chives *(Fall)*

2 (½-inch/12-mm) slices rustic bread
1 ripe avocado, pitted, flesh scooped out, peel discarded
Kosher salt and freshly cracked black pepper
Juice of ½ lemon
2 slices smoked salmon
½ shallot, thinly sliced
Chopped fresh chives or chive blossoms

Toast the bread in a toaster or toaster oven. Smash the avocado in a medium bowl, season with salt and pepper, and add the lemon juice. Top each piece of toast with half of the avocado mixture. Place one slice of smoked salmon over each toast, then add the shallot. Season with salt and pepper and garnish with the chives. Serve immediately.

Serves 2 | Total Time: 5 minutes (Prep: 5. Cook: 0.)

Avocado Toast with Bacon and a Fried Egg *(Winter)*

2 (½-inch/12-mm) slices rustic bread
1 ripe avocado, pitted, flesh scooped out, peel discarded
Kosher salt and freshly cracked black pepper
Juice of ½ lemon
1 teaspoon olive oil
2 large eggs
2 strips bacon, crisped and torn into pieces
Microgreens

Toast the bread in a toaster or toaster oven. Smash the avocado in a medium bowl, season with salt and pepper, and add the lemon juice. Top each piece of toast with half of the avocado mixture. Heat a nonstick skillet over medium-high heat and add the oil. Add the eggs to the skillet and fry until the whites are set and the yolks are cooked to your liking. Place an egg over each piece of toast, then top with the bacon. Season with salt and pepper and garnish with microgreens. Serve immediately.

Serves 2 | Total Time: 8 minutes (Prep: 5. Cook: 3)

Chapter 3:

Bowls

This chapter is my ode to the simple pleasure that is the bowl. A bowl isn't just a serving piece in my kitchen—it's a way of life. It all started when Adam, one of my best friends and food stylist extraordinaire, said he thinks food tastes better when served in a bowl, and he's right! There's something about loading a bowl up with layers of ingredients and mixing them as you eat that's so much more enjoyable than eating from a plate.

Black Rice *and Roasted* Mushroom Bowl

There's a man at the Santa Monica farmers' market who has THE BEST wild mushrooms. Every Wednesday I make a beeline to see what he has and make sure I get dibs, because everyone else is pretty much doing the same thing. I buy a few pounds on the regular, so while they're incredibly delicious simply sautéed, I like to keep things interesting. If I'm feeling jazzy, I'll serve the cooked mushrooms over chewy black rice with herb-loaded salsa verde drizzled over the top along with some slices of avocado and a poached egg. It's a vegetarian dish, but the rich, meaty mushrooms won't leave anyone feeling deprived.

Ingredients

2 cups (400 g) uncooked black rice
6 large eggs
2 recipes Garlic Wild Mushrooms (page 116)
2 ripe avocados, pitted, peeled, and thinly sliced
1 recipe Salsa Verde (page 263)
Kosher salt and freshly cracked black pepper

Cook the rice according to the package directions, then divide among 6 serving bowls.

While the rice is cooking, cook the eggs: Fill a large saucepan with about 4 inches (10 cm) of water. Bring the water to a boil, then lower the heat so that the water simmers gently. Lower in the eggs and set the timer for exactly 6 minutes. Remove the eggs and run them under cold water for 15 seconds. Carefully crack each egg and peel off the membrane and shell. When cut open, the whites should be set and the yolks should be soft and runny. Season with salt and pepper.

Top the rice bowls with equal amounts of the wild mushrooms, avocado, a salsa verde, and a 6-minute egg cut open so the yolk spills out. Serve immediately.

Serves 8 | Total Time: 45 minutes (Prep: 5. Cook: 35.)

Mango Tuna Poke Bowl

Poke is definitely the food of the moment in Los Angeles, and I totally approve. This Hawaiian classic is packed with fresh ingredients like raw fish, pickled veggies, and fruit all heaped over rice and tossed with a soy sauce dressing. So yum.

Ingredients

For the rice:
1 cup (200 g) uncooked short-grain white rice
2 tablespoons rice vinegar

For the soy sauce dressing:
¼ cup (60 ml) soy sauce, or to taste
2 cloves garlic, finely chopped
2 tablespoons rice vinegar
2 tablespoons toasted sesame oil
2 tablespoons olive oil

For the bowls:
3 cups (450 g) cubed sashimi-grade tuna (½-inch/12-mm cubes)
2 ripe avocados, peeled, pitted, and flesh cubed (½-inch/12-mm cubes)
1 cup (155 g) peeled cooked edamame
1 cup (100 g) cubed seedless English cucumber (½-inch/12-mm cubes)
1 cup (165 g) cubed mango (½-inch/12-mm cubes)
½ cup (25 g) sliced scallions (white and light green parts only)
Fresh cilantro leaves
Pickled ginger
Fried wonton strips (optional)

To make the rice: Cook the rice according to the package directions, then toss with the vinegar and divide among 6 serving bowls.

To make the dressing: While the rice is cooking, in a medium bowl, whisk together the soy sauce, garlic, vinegar, sesame oil, and olive oil. Taste and adjust the soy sauce if you want it saltier.

To make the bowls: Top the rice with the assorted toppings in small piles: tuna, avocado, edamame, cucumber, mango, and scallions. Garnish with cilantro, pickled ginger, and fried wonton strips, if using. Drizzle with the dressing and serve.

Serves 6 | Total Time: 25 minutes (Prep: 5. Cook: 20.)

K-Town Beef Bowl *with* Kimchi

One of my favorite neighborhoods to explore in Los Angeles is Koreatown. Okay, if I'm being honest, it took me eight years to FINALLY get there (in my defense, I don't have a car and it's across town!). But once I did, I couldn't stop thinking about beef bulgogi: thin slices of beef that are marinated with garlic, soy sauce, and chile flakes, then griddled to caramelized perfection and served over rice. There is some major K-town inspiration fueling this dish plus an herb salad for maximum freshness.

Ingredients

For the beef:

1 pound (455 g) trimmed hanger steak
3 tablespoons soy sauce
1½ tablespoons toasted sesame oil
2 tablespoons grated peeled ginger
3 cloves garlic, roughly chopped
1 teaspoon crushed red pepper flakes
1 tablespoon light brown sugar
2 tablespoons vegetable oil
Kosher salt

For the quick pickles:

3 Persian cucumbers, thinly sliced
1 carrot, thinly sliced
¼ red onion, finely diced
½ cup (120 ml) rice vinegar

For the scallion salad:

8 scallions, white and light green parts, thinly sliced on the diagonal
1 cup (40 g) fresh cilantro leaves
½ cup (25 g) fresh mint leaves
2 teaspoons toasted sesame oil
1 teaspoon rice vinegar
1 teaspoon sesame seeds
Kosher salt

For serving:

2 cups (410 g) jasmine rice, cooked according to directions, still warm
1 to 2 tablespoons rice vinegar
1 cup (70 g) store-bought kimchi

To make the beef: Freeze the beef for 30 minutes, then use a knife to slice it against the grain into super-thin strips.

Combine the soy sauce, sesame oil, ginger, garlic, red pepper flakes, and brown sugar in a large zip-top bag. Add the beef to the marinade, seal the bag, and mix everything together until evenly coated. Let sit at room temperature for 1 hour, or chill in the refrigerator for up to 8 hours.

To make the quick pickles: In a medium bowl, combine the vegetables and vinegar. Let sit at room temperature for at least 30 minutes, or up to 2 hours.

To make the scallion salad: In a medium bowl, combine the scallions, cilantro, mint, sesame oil, vinegar, and sesame seeds. Season with salt.

To cook the beef: Heat 1 tablespoon of the vegetable oil in a large skillet over medium-high heat. Remove half of the meat from the marinade, letting excess drip back into the bag. Season lightly with salt and cook in a single layer without moving until lightly browned, about 1 minute. Continue to cook, tossing occasionally, until the meat is crisp around the edges, 5 minutes total. Transfer to a plate. Repeat with the remaining 1 tablespoon oil and meat.

To serve: Toss the rice with the rice vinegar. Divide the rice among 4 bowls and top with the quick pickles, beef, scallion salad, and kimchi. Serve immediately.

Serves 4 | Total Time: At least 1 hour and 35 minutes
(Prep: 15. Cook: 20.)

Chimichurri Cauliflower Rice Bowl *with* Grilled Fish

When I'm trying to keep things healthy, cauliflower rice is my fix for getting the rice texture without all those empty calories. It has the same satisfying chew as white rice and also takes on the flavor of anything you pair it with. For this recipe, I teamed it up with mahi mahi, since fish is my go-to when I want a light and quick lunch option. The combo is the perfect palette for Pineapple-Mango Salsa and Salsa Verde (or Basil Vinaigrette—page 250—if I already have a batch made), and the combination of sweet and spicy is so, so good.

Ingredients

4 cups (540 g) cauliflower florets, rinsed and fully dried
1 tablespoon olive oil, plus more for the fish
Kosher salt and freshly cracked black pepper
1 lemon
¼ cup (40 g) Salsa Verde (page 263), plus more if needed
2 pounds (910 g) mahi mahi or cod
2 ripe avocados, pitted, peeled, and sliced or diced
2 cups (330 g) Pineapple-Mango Salsa (page 255)

Place the cauliflower in a food processor and pulse until it has the texture of rice, about 30 seconds. Work in batches if necessary and don't overprocess, or it will get mushy.

In a large skillet, heat the oil over medium heat. Add the cauliflower and cook until heated through, 3 to 4 minutes. Season with salt and pepper and a squeeze of lemon (the lemon helps remove any bitterness from the raw cauliflower). Remove from the skillet to a bowl and toss with the salsa verde. Divide the "rice" among 4 serving bowls.

Preheat an outdoor grill or grill pan over medium-high heat. Drizzle the fish with a touch of oil and liberally season it with salt and pepper.

Grill the fish for 5 to 6 minutes on each side, until the fish is fully cooked, it flakes easily, and has a golden crust. Remove the fish from the grill and squeeze the remaining lemon juice over the fish.

Divide the fish among the cauliflower rice bowls. Top with the avocado and pineapple-mango salsa. Season with salt and pepper and serve.

Serves 4 | Total Time: 20 minutes (Prep: 5. Cook: 15.)

Chicken Larb Bowl *with* Coconut Rice

You've never seen two girls attack a chicken larb situation like me and my friend Mink. It's a traditional Thai salad that just hits all the flavor spots—spicy, meaty, herby, pickle-y. So I had to figure out how to re-create it at home, down to the sticky, sweet coconut rice.

Ingredients

For the quick pickles:
2 Persian cucumbers, thinly sliced
½ red onion, thinly sliced
2 tablespoons rice vinegar

For the chicken:
1 tablespoon vegetable oil
5 ounces (140 g) kale, stems removed, chopped
1¼ (570 g) pounds ground chicken
2 cloves garlic, finely chopped
6 scallions, white and light green parts, thinly sliced
2 to 3 tablespoons soy sauce
1 to 2 tablespoons sambal oelek
1 tablespoon brown sugar

For the rice:
2½ cups (600 ml) water
1 cup (240 ml) coconut milk
1 teaspoon sugar
1 teaspoon kosher salt
2 cups (380 g) jasmine rice
Zest and juice of 1 lime

For the garnishes:
Fresh mint leaves
Fresh basil leaves
Fresh cilantro leaves

To make the quick pickles: In a small bowl, toss the cucumbers, red onion, and vinegar. Set aside to marinate while you cook the chicken.

To make the chicken: In a large, heavy-bottomed skillet, heat the oil over medium-high heat. Add the kale and cook until wilted, 5 to 6 minutes. Season with salt and carefully transfer to a medium bowl.

Add the ground chicken to the same skillet and cook, breaking it apart with the back of a wooden spoon and stirring frequently until no pink remains, 8 to 10 minutes. Add the garlic and scallions and cook for 1 minute, or until fragrant. Add the soy sauce, sambal oelek, and brown sugar and stir to combine. Return the cooked kale into the skillet and stir to combine. Season with salt and reduce the heat to low until ready to serve.

To make the rice: Combine the water, coconut milk, sugar, and salt in a medium saucepan and heat over medium-high heat until the mixture starts to simmer. Add the rice and bring back to a low simmer. Cover the pot, reduce the heat to low, and cook undisturbed for about 15 minutes, until all the liquid as been absorbed. Turn off the heat and let the rice steam for another 5 to 10 minutes until fully cooked and soft. Uncover, fluff, and toss in the lime zest and juice.

To assemble: Divide the rice among 4 bowls, followed by the chicken and kale, pickles, and plenty of fresh mint, basil, and cilantro. Serve immediately.

Serves 4 | Time: 40 minutes (Prep: 10. Cook: 30.)

Green Rice Burrito Bowl

When I was a freshman in college, I went to Chipotle almost every day to get one of their burrito "bowls." Popularly considered a healthier alternative to their ginormous burritos, I thought I was doing myself a favor. But after a year of ordering those heaping mounds of white rice, a week's serving of meat, cheese, and sour cream (who wants veggies when you're stressed and sleep-deprived?!), the freshman fifteen (or twenty, in my case), made their way to my midsection. I needed to figure out how to scratch that itch but not be shoveling in so many calories. I came up with this alternative—a DIY version with brown rice, black beans (my favorite, but you could sub in yours), fresh and spicy pico de gallo, a bit of cheese (just enough to satisfy), colorful romaine and bell peppers, and cilantro vinaigrette, which makes everything a little bit brighter. Oh, and my famous guacamole, because obviously.

Ingredients

2 cups (380 g) uncooked brown basmati rice
Cilantro Vinaigrette (page 251)
1 cup (185 g) cooked black beans
Gaby's Famous Guacamole (page 27)
Pico de Gallo (page 45)
Shredded romaine lettuce
Chopped yellow or orange bell peppers
1½ cups (110 g) shredded Colby-Jack cheese
Chopped fresh cilantro (optional)

Cook the rice according to the package directions, then fold in the vinaigrette.

Divide the rice among 4 bowls and top with the black beans, guacamole, pico de gallo, lettuce, bell peppers, and cheese. Garnish with cilantro if you like and serve.

Serves 4 | Time: 55 minutes (Prep: 15. Cook: 40.)

Chicken Tzatziki Bowl

After spending last summer in Greece with our dear friends Heather and Pete and their kids (who are also my spirit animals), I now look for any excuse to eat tzatziki, a creamy, tangy yogurt sauce perfumed with fresh dill. It's great on salads, as a veggie dip, or slathered over meats. This bowl pretty much hits all three, with smoky yogurt-marinated grilled chicken heaped over quinoa and Mediterranean-inspired tomatoes, cucumbers, and olives. You'll need eight wooden or metal skewers for this recipe (and make sure to soak wooden skewers in water for about 30 minutes before using).

Ingredients

For the chicken:

2 pounds (910 g) boneless, skinless chicken thighs
½ cup (120 ml) full-fat plain Greek yogurt
1 tablespoon olive oil
1 tablespoon red wine vinegar
4 cloves garlic, finely chopped
1 teaspoon dried oregano
1 teaspoon ground turmeric
1 teaspoon kosher salt, plus more for sprinkling
½ teaspoon red pepper flakes
Freshly cracked black pepper

For the salad:

2 tablespoons olive oil
1 tablespoon red wine vinegar
Kosher salt and freshly cracked black pepper
3 Persian cucumbers, thinly sliced
1 cup (145 g) cherry tomatoes, halved
¼ red onion, thinly sliced

For the bowls:

4 cups (805 g) cooked quinoa
1 cup (270 ml) Cucumber Dill Tzatziki (page 32)
1 cup (150 g) authentic feta (the kind that comes in brine), crumbled
12 to 16 crushed castelvetrano olives

To make the chicken: Cut the chicken thighs into 1-inch (2.5-cm) pieces. In a large bowl, whisk together the yogurt, oil, vinegar, garlic, oregano, turmeric, salt, and red pepper flakes. Add the chicken and stir to coat. Cover and marinate in the refrigerator for at least 1 hour and up to 8 hours.

Preheat an outdoor grill or grill pan to medium-high heat. Thread the chicken pieces among 8 wooden or metal skewers, discarding the marinade in the bowl. Sprinkle with salt and pepper.

Grill the chicken, turning the skewers occasionally, until golden brown and cooked through, 10 to 12 minutes total.

To make the salad: In a medium bowl, whisk together the oil and vinegar and season with salt and pepper. Add the cucumbers, cherry tomatoes, and red onion and toss to combine.

To make the bowls: Divide the quinoa among 4 bowls. Top with the cucumber salad, followed by a spoonful of tzatziki, 2 to 3 tablespoons crumbled feta, and 3 or 4 olives. Top with 2 chicken skewers and serve immediately.

Serves: 4 | Total Time: At least 1 hour and 25 minutes
(Prep: 10. Cook: 15.)

Chapter 4:

Give Me All the Greens!

If there's one thing that California does really, really well—besides yoga pants—it's produce. It's just about impossible to go to the market and not get inspired by all the fruits and veggies on offer. And in order to preserve all their natural flavor, I want to do as little to them as possible. That said, "simple" doesn't have to mean a sad bowl of lettuce, cucumbers, and tomatoes. This chapter is all about the art of the salad, or creating layers of flavor and texture that let all the ingredients shine.

Sesame-Miso Market Salad

This recipe is inspired by one of my best friends, Catherine, who has a serious fling going on with a sesame-miso dressing that she buys at the Hollywood Farmers' Market. Every time I go to her house, she serves a salad tossed with it. And I can tell you that her obsession is totally worthwhile because this dressing is one of the best I've ever had—creamy, salty, sweet—all the tastes and feels that you want in a salad. I was on a mission to re-create it at home, and when I cracked the code, you better bet this made its way onto just about every veggie that entered my house.

Ingredients

For the sesame-miso dressing:

1½ tablespoons miso paste
2 tablespoons rice vinegar
1 tablespoon honey
1 tablespoon grated ginger
1 clove garlic, finely chopped
1 tablespoon toasted sesame oil
1 tablespoon soy sauce
1½ teaspoons fresh lime juice
1 teaspoon toasted sesame seeds
Salt and freshly cracked black pepper to taste

For the salad:

4 to 6 cups (160 to 240 g) assorted greens
1 Asian pear, cored and thinly sliced
2 Persian cucumbers, thinly sliced
1 ripe avocado, pitted, peeled, and thinly sliced or diced
2 mandarin oranges, peeled and segmented
Kosher salt and freshly cracked black pepper to taste

To make the dressing: Combine all the ingredients in a mason jar, cover, and shake. Adjust the salt and pepper as needed.

To make the salad: Combine all the ingredients in a large serving bowl. Drizzle with ¼ cup (60 ml) of the dressing and toss to combine. Taste and add more dressing and more salt and pepper if needed. Serve immediately.

Serves 8 | Total Time: 10 minutes (Prep: 10. Cook: 0.)

Grilled Radicchio Salad

You'll barely find me in the kitchen in the summer. That's because I basically live outside—whether it's on my patio, in Matt and Adam's incredible backyard, in Malibu by the beach, or anywhere else with a chair and umbrella. Especially in California, it's just too damn nice to be spending a lot of time inside cooking. But there's no way I'd take a season off from making food, so I take the kitchen outside with me (hello, grill) and also stick to dishes that don't need a ton of prep. This salad checks both boxes, giving a smokiness to the radicchio that pairs so perfectly with sweet citrus, salty prosciutto, and blue cheese.

Ingredients

For the citrus-fennel vinaigrette:

¼ cup (60 ml) fresh orange juice
2 tablespoons fresh lemon juice
1 tablespoon Champagne vinegar
1 teaspoon Dijon mustard
⅓ cup (75 ml) olive oil
1 shallot, finely minced
1 teaspoon fennel seeds, toasted and crushed
1 clove garlic, minced
Kosher salt and freshly cracked black pepper to taste

For the salad:

8 thin slices prosciutto
2 heads radicchio, cut into quarters
Olive oil
Kosher salt and freshly cracked black pepper
2 large navel oranges, peeled and sliced
½ cup (85 g) toasted hazelnuts, crushed
2 ounces (55 g) crumbled blue cheese

To make the vinaigrette: Combine all the ingredients in a medium bowl and whisk to combine. Taste and adjust salt and pepper as needed.

To make the salad: Heat a large nonstick skillet over medium-high heat. Carefully place 4 pieces of the prosciutto in the skillet and cook for 2 minutes on each side, until the prosciutto shrinks considerably and crisps up. Remove from the skillet and transfer to a clean surface. Repeat with the remaining prosciutto.

Preheat an outdoor grill or grill pan to high heat. Brush all cut sides of the radicchio with oil and season with salt and pepper. Place the radicchio on the grill cut side down and grill for 2 minutes per side, until just slightly charred and softened. Remove from the grill and place on a serving platter. Arrange the orange slices over and around the radicchio. Sprinkle with the toasted hazelnuts, crumble the crisped prosciutto on top, and finish with the crumbled blue cheese. Drizzle heavily with the vinaigrette and serve immediately.

Serves 8 | Total Time: 25 minutes (Prep: 15. Cook: 10.)

Cobb for All Seasons

Confession time: I'm not a fan of traditional Cobb salad. Hard-boiled egg? Heck no. Blue cheese dressing? Absolutely not. They're just not my jam. But I do love the idea of an enormous salad that's stuffed with all kinds of goodies, so I created my own version of the Cobb for each season. Trust me, these aren't your average wimpy, leafy green salads. I've loaded up these twists on a classic with hearty, substantial ingredients that vibe with whatever's fresh at the market: radishes and artichokes for spring, corn and chipotle chicken for summer, sweet potatoes and beets for fall, and gorgeous pomegranates and crispy croutons for winter. These salads stand alone as a main dish, play well with others as a side, and pack up perfectly to take to the office. I love making one on a Sunday and then working through it all week (just hold off on adding the dressing until you're ready to dig in).

Spring Cobb with Asparagus, Artichokes, and Avocado

8 heads little gem lettuce, bottom 1 inch (2.5 cm) trimmed off and separated into individual leaves
4 Persian cucumbers, thinly sliced on a diagonal
1 Easter radish, very thinly sliced
1 ripe avocado, pitted, peeled, and thinly sliced
3 tablespoons chopped fresh dill
3 tablespoons chopped fresh mint
8 canned artichoke hearts, drained and halved
12 ounces roasted asparagus (page 124), cut into 2-inch (5-cm) pieces
Lemon-Champagne Vinaigrette (page 251)
Kosher salt and freshly cracked black pepper

Arrange the lettuce leaves in a large salad bowl. Top with the sliced cucumbers, radish, avocado, dill, mint, artichoke hearts, and roasted asparagus. Toss with the lemon-champagne vinaigrette and season with salt and pepper. Serve immediately.

Serves 4 to 6 | Total Time: 10 minutes (Prep: 10. Cook: 0.)

Summer Chipotle Chicken Cobb

For the chicken:

1 tablespoon vegetable oil
2 chipotle chiles in adobo, finely chopped
1 teaspoon garlic powder
1 teaspoon ground cumin
½ teaspoon dried oregano
½ teaspoon freshly cracked black pepper
4 boneless, skinless chicken thighs (or 3 boneless, skinless chicken breasts)

For the salad:

3 to 4 cups (120 to 160 g) market greens
4 strips applewood-smoked bacon, cooked and crumbled
8 to 10 strawberries, hulled and quartered
2 ears corn on the cob, kernels removed in strips
1 to 2 ripe avocados, pitted, peeled, and sliced
Kosher salt and freshly cracked black pepper
Lemon-Champagne Vinaigrette (page 251)

To make the chicken: Combine the oil, chipotles, garlic powder, cumin, oregano, and black pepper in a small bowl. Place the chicken in a large zip-top bag and add the marinade. Zip the bag and mix the chicken into the marinade to coat. Place in the fridge and let it marinate for at least 1 hour and up to 8 hours.

Heat an outdoor grill or grill pan to about 400°F (205°C) (medium-high heat). Place the chicken on the grill and grill for 5 to 6 minutes per side, until the chicken is cooked through. Remove the chicken from the grill and let rest for 10 minutes. Slice the chicken against the grain.

Arrange the greens on a large platter and top with the bacon, strawberries, corn, avocado, and grilled chicken and season with salt and pepper. Toss with the vinaigrette and serve.

Serves 4 to 6 | Total Time: At least 1 hour and 30 minutes (Prep: 10. Cook: 10.)

Fall Cobb with Sweet Potatoes and Beets

3 medium sweet potatoes, peeled and cut into ½-inch (12-mm) cubes
2 tablespoons olive oil
Kosher salt and freshly cracked black pepper
3 to 4 heads romaine lettuce, cut into ¾-inch (2-cm) ribbons
4 cooked beets, halved or quartered
1 cup (145 g) heirloom cherry tomatoes, halved
2 ripe avocados, pitted, peeled, and chopped
1 cup (160 g) canned chickpeas, rinsed and drained
Mustard-Herb Vinaigrette (page 252)

In a large bowl, toss the cubed sweet potatoes with the oil and season with salt and pepper. Spread out over a parchment-lined baking sheet and roast for about 25 minutes, tossing occasionally, until softened and browned. Remove from the heat and let cool.

Arrange the lettuce on a large platter and top with the sweet potatoes, beets, cherry tomatoes, avocado, and chickpeas. Toss with the vinaigrette and serve.

Serves 4 to 6 | Total Time: 35 minutes
(Prep: 10. Cook: 25.)

Winter Cobb with Pomegranates

For the croutons:
½ loaf French bread (a few days old)
3 tablespoons olive oil
3 tablespoons unsalted butter, melted
4 cloves garlic, chopped
2 teaspoons kosher salt
1 teaspoon freshly cracked black pepper
1 teaspoon dried Italian seasoning

For the salad:
8 ounces baby kale
1 cup (180 g) pomegranate seeds
2 Persian cucumbers, sliced
2 Satsuma mandarin oranges
4 ounces pancetta, crisped
1 Honeycrisp apple, cored and cubed
1 Bosc pear, cored and cubed
1 Fuyu persimmon, cored and cubed (optional)
Lemon-Champagne Vinaigrette (page 251)
Kosher salt and freshly cracked black pepper

To make the croutons: Preheat the oven to 350°F (175°C). Line a baking sheet with parchment paper.

Rip the bread into small pieces and place them in a bowl. Drizzle the bread with the olive oil and butter, then add the garlic, salt, pepper, and Italian seasoning. Using your hands, gently toss the croutons to evenly coat them with the oil, butter, and seasonings. Transfer the croutons to the prepared baking sheet and bake for 15 to 20 minutes, tossing with a pair of tongs halfway through, until golden brown. Remove from the oven and let cool before serving.

To make the salad: Make a bed of kale in a large salad bowl or platter. Pile on the pomegranate seeds, cucumbers, mandarins, pancetta, apple, pear, persimmon, and 1 cup (40 g) of the croutons (reserve the extra croutons for another use). Toss with the vinaigrette, season with salt and pepper, and serve.

Serves 4 to 6 | Total Time: 25 to 30 minutes
(Prep: 10. Cook: 15 to 20.)

Winter Citrus Salad

Not to rub it in that California is the sunniest, lushest produce capital of the United States (though let's be honest, it is!), but there is nothing quite like the citrus here. When the winter produce situation just about everywhere else is starting to look a little bleak, our trees are exploding with lemons, grapefruits, and oranges that come in all shapes, sizes, and flavors. Luckily, most grocery stores offer a decent selection of these California exports, so you should be able to find delicious varieties near you. And if you're going to use the freshest, most delicious fruit in a salad, then there's no sense in covering it up with a whole bunch of overpowering ingredients. That's why I pair it with some tangy goat cheese, pistachios for crunch, and a drizzle of champagne vinaigrette to bring out the sweet, tart notes of the fruits and tie the whole dish together. It's the ultimate dish for snagging a little California sun on a cold winter day.

Ingredients

2 blood oranges
2 Cara Cara oranges
2 tangerines
1 pink grapefruit
1 navel orange
¼ cup (30 g) chopped pistachios
¼ cup (30 g) crumbled soft goat cheese
Maldon sea salt
Lemon-Champagne Vinaigrette (page 251)

Using a sharp paring knife, cut a thin slice off the top and bottom end of each piece of citrus. Stand one up on a clean work surface. Working from the top to the bottom of the fruit, cut off the peel and white pith in wide strips, following the contour of the fruit. Flip the fruit over and trim away any white pith on the other end. Repeat with the remaining citrus, then cut the fruits crosswise into ¼-inch (6-mm) thick slices and remove the seeds.

Layer the sliced citrus on a large serving platter. Top with the pistachios and goat cheese and sprinkle with salt. Drizzle with the lemon-champagne vinaigrette and serve immediately.

Serves 4 to 6 | Total Time: 10 minutes (Prep: 10. Cook: 0.)

Southwestern Cowboy Caviar Salad

This salad looks back to my days of being an Arizona girl, when cowboy caviar—as my mom called black beans—was served on the regular. This classic Southwest combo adds corn, bell peppers, and avocado to the mix and involves zero cooking, which makes it perfect for nights when you're 1) in a rush, 2) too lazy to cook, or 3) it's too hot to turn on the oven.

Ingredients

2 heads romaine or little gem lettuce
1 head frisée
1½ cups (275 g) cooked black beans, drained
1 cup (145 g) raw corn kernels, sliced off the cob
½ yellow bell pepper, sliced
½ red bell pepper, sliced
½ orange bell pepper, sliced
2 large ripe avocados, peeled, pitted, and cubed
Kosher salt and freshly cracked black pepper
Cilantro Vinaigrette (page 251)

On a large platter, combine the lettuce, frisée, black beans, corn, bell peppers, and avocados. Season with salt and pepper, drizzle with cilantro vinaigrette, and serve.

Serves 4 to 6 | Total Time: 10 minutes (Prep: 10. Cook: 0.)

Mom's Every Night Cucumber Salad

As you probably guessed from the name of the recipe, my mom made this salad just about every night when I was growing up. It was so yummy that I'd eat half the bowl before we even sat down for dinner, even though I'd get yelled at for not saving any for my dad and sister. Hey, a girl's gotta look out for herself! Now it's my go-to side salad, and my husband eats half of it before we sit down for dinner. Apparently that whole what-goes-around-comes-around situation is really a thing.

Ingredients

3 tablespoons olive oil
2 tablespoons balsamic vinegar
2 cloves garlic, finely chopped
Kosher salt and freshly cracked black pepper
1 ripe avocado, pitted, peeled, and sliced or diced
4 Persian cucumbers, sliced
1 to 2 cups (20 to 40 g) arugula (optional)
½ cup (75 g) halved cherry tomatoes (optional)

In a medium bowl, whisk together the oil, balsamic vinegar, and garlic. Season with salt and pepper. Add the avocado and cucumbers to the bowl and toss to combine. Serve immediately.

Serves 4 | Total Time: 3 minutes (Prep: 2. Cook: 0.)

Chapter 5:

Things to Put on the Side

When you cook with fresh produce at the peak of its seasonality, it doesn't need a whole lot besides tender love and care. So all that stands between you and a whole bunch of delicious, versatile side dishes are a few high-quality ingredients and simple techniques for cooking veggies perfectly.

Stone Fruit *with* Burrata

There's never been a match made in heaven like this side—perfectly ripe nectarines, peaches, pluots, and plums plus creamy, rich burrata cheese and a light, bright lemon vinaigrette. Serve it on its own as a side or on a bed of arugula as a salad.

Ingredients

1 white nectarine, pitted and cut into wedges
1 yellow nectarine, pitted and cut into wedges
1 white peach, pitted and cut into wedges
1 yellow peach, pitted and cut into wedges
2 plums, pitted and cut into wedges
2 pluots, pitted and cut into wedges
8 ounces (225 g) burrata cheese
Maldon sea salt and freshly cracked black pepper
Fresh basil leaves
Lemon-Champagne Vinaigrette (page 251)

Arrange the stone fruit on a large plate or bowl. Carefully rip the ball of burrata into pieces and scatter it on top of the fruit. Sprinkle with salt and pepper, scatter on the basil, drizzle with the lemon-champagne vinaigrette, and serve.

Serves 6 to 8 | Total Time: 5 minutes (Prep: 5. Cook: 0.)

Thyme and Garlic Marinated Peppers

My Papa (my mom's dad) makes the most epic old school–style Bulgarian pepper salad. The minute I'm on the plane to visit him in Florida, I'm already thinking about eating this dish. He roasts bell peppers on the grill, then wraps them in newspaper to sweat them (told you it was old-school!). He skins the peppers, ditches the seeds, then whips up a simple vinaigrette to pour over the top and lets the peppers soak for just enough time to take on all that flavor. Papa—a self-proclaimed pepper fanatic—will eat the peppers whole, but I like serving them in strips, which makes a great side for grilled meats or a topper for good crusty bread.

Ingredients

2 yellow bell peppers
2 orange bell peppers
2 red bell peppers
¼ red onion, thinly sliced
2 large cloves garlic, thinly sliced
2 tablespoons red wine vinegar
3 tablespoons olive oil
2 teaspoon chopped fresh thyme
Kosher salt and freshly cracked black pepper

Preheat an outdoor grill or grill pan to medium-high heat.

Place the yellow, orange, and red peppers directly on the grill and char on all sides until the skin is black all over, 10 to 15 minutes (see Note). Remove the peppers from the grill, place them in a glass bowl, cover with plastic wrap, and let steam for 20 minutes.

Carefully peel the charred skin off the peppers. Slice the peppers in half lengthwise and remove the ribs and seeds. Cut into 1-inch (2.5-cm) wide strips and transfer to a serving bowl. Add the red onion, garlic, vinegar, oil, and thyme and season with salt and pepper. Toss to combine and let marinate for at least 30 minutes and up to 3 hours. Serve immediately, or transfer to a jar and keep refrigerated until ready to serve.

Serves 6 to 8 | Total Time: At least 1 hour and 5 minutes (Prep: 5. Cook: 10 to 15.)

Note: **Alternatively, you could roast the peppers in the oven. Preheat the oven to 425°F (220°C). Place the peppers on a foil-lined baking sheet and roast, turning occasionally, until the peppers are charred, 30 to 35 minutes.**

Lemon Shishito Peppers

When the shishito peppers start showing up at the farmers' market, it's cause for a party—literally. Even though I rarely make appetizers unless people are coming over, shishito season is a different story. My husband and I buy them by the carload and cook this dish every night until we run out. They have so much natural flavor that it doesn't take much to make them taste delicious—just sautéing them, sprinkling with salt, and drizzling with lemon juice and olive oil. Eating them is like Russian roulette, because one in every ten or so is super-spicy.

Ingredients

1 tablespoon vegetable oil
1 pound (455 g) shishito peppers (or padrón peppers if in season)
Maldon sea salt
1 tablespoon extra-virgin olive oil
1 lemon

Heat the vegetable oil in a large cast-iron skillet over high heat until it starts to smoke. Add the shishito peppers and cook, tossing often, until they are blistered on both sides, 3 to 5 minutes. Remove the peppers from the pan to a bowl. Season with salt, drizzle with olive oil, and squeeze with lemon. Serve warm.

Serves 4 | Total Time: 5 minutes (Prep: 0. Cook: 5.)

Watermelon and Heirloom Tomato Caprese

Trying to choose between watermelon and cherries as my favorite summer fruit would be like picking a favorite child from my nonexistent children—don't make me do it! But for the sake of this salad, I'll let watermelon take the spotlight. I love making sweet-savory salads with this juicy summer staple along with heirloom tomatoes and fresh mozzarella. Some basil, salt, pepper, and a balsamic glaze over the top and your backyard BBQ is done and done. If you can find yellow watermelon, which has just a little more perfume than its pink cousins, try it instead.

Ingredients

3 to 4 small green zebra tomatoes, halved
½ cup (75 g) heirloom cherry tomatoes, halved
1 to 2 cups (150 to 300 g) balled (1-inch/2.5-cm balls) red seedless watermelon
1 to 2 cups (150 to 300 g) balled (1-inch/2.5-cm balls) yellow seedless watermelon
12 ounces (340 g) Bocconcini
10 to 15 small fresh basil leaves
Maldon sea salt and freshly cracked black pepper
Balsamic glaze

In a large bowl, combine the tomatoes, watermelon, and cheese, then transfer to a serving platter or individual glasses. Tear the basil on top, sprinkle with salt and pepper, drizzle with balsamic glaze, and serve.

Serves 4 to 6 | Total Time: 10 minutes (Prep: 10. Cook: 0.)

Pesto Broccolini

Given the option to eat broccoli or broccolini, I always choose the 'lini. Those long, crunchy, leggy stalks are just so elegant and lovely. (Though, truth be told, broccoli is just as delicious, and in a blind taste test, I'm not sure I could even tell the difference!) As if I needed any more reason to love broccolini, I had this incredible flavor combination when I was in Brazil, and my mind was blown—who puts pesto on broccolini, let alone in Brazil?! So brilliant! The first order of business when I got home was to whip up a batch of (just happens to be vegan) pesto-inspired dressing, which has become a multipurpose kitchen workhorse that brightens up just about anything. This dish is a serious addiction in my house, so I'll gladly eat it on its own for dinner, but for those less broccolini fanatical, it makes a great side dish for chicken or fish or an instant lunch bowl when heaped on top of quinoa.

Ingredients

2 tablespoons olive oil
2 pounds (910 g) broccolini, ends trimmed
2 cloves garlic, minced
½ to 1 teaspoon red pepper flakes
Kosher salt and freshly cracked black pepper
½ cup (120 ml) Basil Vinaigrette (page 250)
Lemon wedges

Heat the oil in a large skillet over medium-high heat. Add the broccolini and cook for 6 to 8 minutes until just started to blister on the edges. Add the garlic and red pepper flakes and stir to combine. Continue to cook until the broccolini is just tender, 2 to 4 minutes more. Season with salt and pepper, toss with the basil vinaigrette, and serve immediately with lemon wedges alongside.

Serves 4 to 6 | Total Time: 15 minutes (Prep: 3. Cook: 12.)

Omi's Haricots Verts Salad

Omi, my German grandma, is an incredible cook, and this is one of my favorite dishes that she makes. You know it's a solid green bean salad when you're willing to eat about a pound of it on any given day. And yet it's so simple—just fresh haricots verts tossed with red wine vinegar, olive oil, shallots, garlic, salt, and pepper. You can use green beans if that's all you can find, but haricots verts—their longer, leaner counterpart—are more delicate and pretty.

Ingredients

1 pound (455 g) haricots verts, ends trimmed
2 tablespoons red wine vinegar
3 tablespoons olive oil
1 shallot, thinly sliced
2 cloves garlic, finely chopped
Kosher salt and freshly cracked black pepper

Bring a large pot of water to boil. Add the haricots verts and blanch for 6 to 7 minutes—they should be crisp but tender. Drain and set aside.

In a large bowl, whisk together the vinegar, oil, shallot, and garlic and season with salt and pepper. Add the haricots verts to the vinaigrette and toss to combine. Let sit for 20 minutes, then adjust the salt and pepper if needed. Serve warm, chilled, or at room temperature.

Serves 4 | Total Time: About 30 minutes (Prep: 3. Cook: 7.)

Charred Sugar Snap Peas

One of the easiest ways to get more complex flavor from your vegetables is to sear them hard in a super-hot cast-iron skillet. Sugar snap peas are perfect candidates for this smoky treatment, then I top them with mint, a classic combination for spring.

Ingredients

1 tablespoon olive oil
1 pound (455 g) sugar snap peas, trimmed
1 teaspoon red pepper flakes
Zest and juice of 1 to 2 lemons
½ cup (25 g) torn fresh mint leaves
Maldon sea salt

Heat the oil in a large cast-iron skillet over medium-high heat. Add the sugar snap peas, tossing them to mix into the oil and scattering them over the pan. Cook for about 2 minutes, until they start to blister and char on the bottom. Using tongs, toss and cook for about 2 minutes longer, until nicely charred all over.

Remove the sugar snap peas to a large bowl, add the red pepper flakes, lemon zest and juice, and the mint and toss to combine. Season with salt and serve.

Serves 4 to 6 | Total Time: 8 minutes (Prep: 4. Cook: 4.)

Perfect Roasted Potatoes

There's nothing more depressing than a roasted potato that's fluffy and creamy in the middle but not caramelized and crispy on the outside. So here's the trick to nailing it every time: plenty of seasoning, roasting, tossing, and hot heat. These are perfect for making in large batches and reheating later (as we do all the time in our house). Serve them as a side, wrap 'em up in a breakfast burrito (page 45), or drizzle them with ketchup and consider them dinner. Don't worry about peeling the potatoes; just make sure to clean them well before chopping them.

Ingredients

4 or 5 large Yukon Gold potatoes (4 to 5 pounds/1.8 to 2.3 kg), cut into ½-inch (12-mm) cubes
3 tablespoons olive oil
2½ teaspoons paprika
1 teaspoon garlic salt
1 teaspoon kosher salt
¾ teaspoon freshly cracked black pepper

Preheat the oven to 425°F (220°C). Line a baking sheet with parchment paper.

Place the potatoes onto the prepared baking sheet. Toss the potatoes with the oil, paprika, garlic salt, kosher salt, and pepper until the seasonings are evenly combined.

Transfer the baking sheet to the oven and bake for 20 minutes. Remove from the oven and toss the potatoes with tongs. Put the baking sheet back in the oven and bake for an additional 20 minutes. Remove the baking sheet, give the potatoes a final toss, place them back in the oven, and roast until they are golden and crispy, 10 to 15 minutes more.

Remove from the oven, adjust the salt if needed, and serve.

Serves 4 to 6 | Total Time: 1 hour (Prep: 5. Cook: 50 to 55.)

Garlic *Wild* Mushrooms

During the third week of culinary school, we learned all about vegetables, and our instructor assigned each of us one to cook with. Mine was mushrooms, and I was petrified—I'd never tried mushrooms, ever, and they scared me. Our instructor looked at me and said, "If you can't wrap your head around mushrooms, you'll never make it as a chef." To that I said, "Okay, WATCH ME" (I love a challenge), and I made the most epic mushrooms ever. I learned that mushrooms don't need much to realize their full earthy, meaty potential—just plenty of space in the pan, tons of heat, a decent amount of fat, and some lemon juice at the end to give them a pop of freshness. I've been hooked ever since.

Ingredients

4 tablespoons (60 ml) olive oil
1½ pounds (680 g) wild mushrooms, ends trimmed and dirt brushed off
½ teaspoon kosher salt
¼ teaspoon freshly cracked black pepper
4 large cloves garlic, chopped
2 tablespoons roughly chopped flat-leaf parsley
1½ tablespoons fresh lemon juice, or to taste
Maldon sea salt

Heat a large, heavy skillet over medium-high heat until hot. Add 3 tablespoons of the oil, then add the mushrooms and cook, stirring frequently, until golden brown, 12 to 14 minutes. Add the kosher salt and pepper.

Add the remaining 1 tablespoon oil, the garlic, and parsley and cook, stirring, until fragrant, about 1 minute. Add the lemon juice and remove from the heat. Add a little Maldon sea salt, taste, and adjust the seasonings as needed. Serve immediately.

Serves 4 | Total Time: 20 minutes (Prep: 5. Cook: 15.)

Tip: **Never rinse a mushroom to clean it. It will soak up too much water. Instead, just use a damp paper towel to gently brush any dirt off the top of the mushroom before chopping and cooking.**

Balsamic Beets *with* Goat Cheese *and* Pistachios

All of the veggie recipes in this book are super-simple, and it's for a reason: when you cook vegetables well and let their natural flavors shine, they don't get much better than that. These beets are no exception. They get tossed with a light dressing plus some goat cheese and nuts. Easy peasy.

Ingredients

6 to 9 medium beets (red or yellow)
2 tablespoons olive oil
½ cup (55 g) crumbled soft goat cheese
½ cup (55 g) chopped lightly salted pistachios
Balsamic Vinaigrette (page 250)
Kosher salt and freshly cracked black pepper

Preheat the oven to 425°F (220°C).

Trim the greens off the beets entirely. Scrub the beets thoroughly, drizzle them with the oil, then loosely wrap them in foil.

Transfer the wrapped beets to a baking sheet and roast for 1 hour, then check for doneness. The beets are done when a fork or skewer slides easily into the middle of a beet. If after 1 hour the beets are not done, continue to roast for 10 minute intervals.

Remove the beets from the oven and let the beets cool slightly. Then, using a paper towel, rub the skin off. The skin should peel away easily; if it doesn't, the beets likely need to roast for a little longer. Cut the beets in halves or quarters. Transfer the beets to a serving platter, top with the goat cheese and pistachios, and drizzle with the balsamic vinaigrette. Season with salt and pepper and serve immediately.

Serves 4 to 6 | Total Time: 1 hour and 5 minutes (Prep: 5. Cook: 1 hour.)

Crispy Brussels Sprouts

This is the dish that will change the mind of every Brussels sprout skeptic out there. I made these for Thanksgiving a few years ago and my uncle gave me total side-eye. I told him to chill, and, lo and behold, he had four servings of them. I just sat back and smiled because I was right. As usual.

Ingredients

¼ cup (60 ml) olive oil
1 teaspoon fresh thyme leaves, roughly chopped
½ teaspoon red pepper flakes
1½ pounds (680 g) Brussels sprouts, trimmed and halved
2 cloves garlic, chopped
½ to 1 whole lemon
Kosher salt and freshly cracked black pepper

In a large skillet combine the oil, thyme, and red pepper flakes and heat over medium-high heat for about 1 minute, until fragrant.

Add the Brussels sprouts and cook for 12 to 15 minutes, until golden brown, stirring frequently to make sure they cook evenly. A minute before the Brussels sprouts are done, add the garlic and stir to combine. Remove from the heat, squeeze in the juice from ½ lemon, and season with salt and pepper. Taste and adjust the lemon juice, salt, and pepper as needed. Serve immediately.

Serves 4 to 6 | Total Time: 20 minutes (Prep: 5. Cook: 15.)

Delicata Squash *with* Pomegranate Seeds

This dish not only is a heavenly combination of creamy, sweet roasted squash and tart pomegranate seeds, but it's also one of the prettiest dishes I've ever come up with. It's perfect for fall or winter entertaining. Because squash can be stored pretty much indefinitely in a cool, dark place, I recommend buying a bunch of delicata squash so you always have one at the ready to make this.

Ingredients

2 delicata squash, seeds removed, flesh cut into ¼-inch (6-mm) rounds
3 tablespoons olive oil
Kosher salt and freshly cracked black pepper
1 teaspoon red pepper flakes
1 tablespoon balsamic glaze
1 cup (180 g) pomegranate seeds
½ cup (55 g) crumbled goat cheese

Preheat the oven to 425°F (220°C). Line a baking sheet with parchment paper.

Place the delicata squash on the prepared baking sheet. Drizzle with the oil, season with salt and pepper, and add the red pepper flakes. Toss to combine. Roast for 25 minutes, or until fork tender.

Remove the baking sheet from the oven and transfer the squash to a serving platter. Drizzle with the balsamic glaze and sprinkle with the pomegranate seeds and goat cheese. Adjust the salt and pepper as needed. Serve immediately. This dish also can be served at room temperature or cold.

Serves 4 to 6 | Total Time: 30 minutes (Prep: 5. Cook: 25.)

Roasted Asparagus with Salsa Verde

Simply roasted veg + staple sauce = home run every time. If you don't have herbes de Provence you can just throw together a combo of equal parts dried rosemary, thyme, and oregano.

Ingredients

2 pounds (910 g) asparagus, ends trimmed
1 tablespoon olive oil
Kosher salt and freshly cracked black pepper
1 teaspoon herbes de Provence
Zest and juice of 1 lemon, plus extra lemon wedges
Salsa Verde (page 263)

Preheat the oven to 425°F (220°C).

Lay the asparagus on a baking sheet, drizzle with the oil, and sprinkle with salt and pepper. Sprinkle with the herbes de Provence and place in the oven. Roast for about 15 minutes, until just tender.

Remove the baking sheet from the oven, drizzle with lemon juice, and dust with the lemon zest. Transfer the asparagus to a serving platter and drizzle the salsa verde on top. Serve with extra lemon wedges.

Serves 4 to 6 | Total Time: 17 minutes (Prep: 2. Cook: 15.)

Chapter 6:

It's Six O'Clock + I'm STARVING

No matter how much you love spending time in the kitchen, there will always be those nights when you have to get dinner on the table FAST. These are my favorite quick-fix recipes for whipping up something delicious in a pinch. Consider them your go-to for easy weeknight meals or for feeding a crowd at a moment's notice.

Lazy Girl Chicken Enchiladas *with* Cumin Crema

If I don't have any time to get dinner on the table, it's all about a store-bought rotisserie chicken. I'll have Thomas grab one on his way home from work, shred it up, and turn it into enchiladas. Thirty-ish minutes later, dinner is done. The cumin crema is what makes these super-special, plus plenty of cheese, beans, and scallions for a splash of color.

Ingredients

For the enchiladas:

2 tablespoons olive oil
1 yellow onion, chopped
1 (4-ounce/115-g) can diced green chiles
½ teaspoon ground cumin
½ teaspoon garlic powder
½ teaspoon red pepper flakes
Salt
1½ cups (295 g) shredded rotisserie chicken
1 (15.5-ounce/445-g) can store-bought enchilada sauce (red or green)
10 large flour tortillas
1 (15.5-ounce/445-g) can refried black or pinto beans
1 cup (115 g) pepper Jack cheese
1 cup (112 g) Mexican-blend shredded cheese
8 scallions, white and light green parts, thinly sliced
Chopped fresh cilantro leaves

For the cumin crema:

¼ cup (60 ml) sour cream
½ teaspoon ground cumin

Preheat the oven to 350°F (175°C).

To make the enchiladas: In a large skillet, heat the oil over medium-high heat. Add the onion and cook for 5 to 7 minutes, until softened. Stir in the diced green chiles, cumin, garlic powder, and red pepper flakes. Season with salt. Stir in the shredded chicken and ½ cup (120 ml) of the enchilada sauce. Remove from the heat.

To assemble the enchiladas, set up an assembly line including tortillas, enchilada sauce, beans, chicken mixture, both of the cheeses mixed together, and scallions. Lay out a tortilla on a flat surface and spoon 1 tablespoon of the refried beans in a line down the center of the tortilla. Add equal amounts of the shredded chicken mixture, 2 tablespoons of cheese, and 1 tablespoon of the scallions, and roll them up. Repeat with the remaining tortillas and fillings.

Pour another ½ cup (120 ml) of the enchilada sauce in the bottom of a 9 by 13-inch (23 by 33-cm) baking dish and place the rolled-up tortillas in the dish. Spread the remaining enchilada sauce on top of the tortillas and sprinkle on the remaining shredded cheese. Bake uncovered for 20 to 25 minutes until the cheese is melted and bubbly.

To make the cumin crema: Stir together the sour cream and cumin in a bowl. Remove the enchiladas from the oven and serve immediately, garnished with the remaining scallions, some cilantro, and a drizzle of cumin crema.

Serves 5 (2 enchiladas each) | Total Time: 35 to 40 minutes (Prep: 10. Cook: 25 to 30.)

Roasted Mushroom *and* Onion Quesadillas

Every day after school I would make my sister and myself a few quesadillas in the microwave. It wasn't exactly gourmet, but I did discover the ideal cheese-to-tortilla ratio so that there would be oozing cheese with every bite. These days I've graduated from cheese-only status to adding some sautéed mushrooms and a sprinkling of cilantro plus a side of salsa and guac. While I'm personally all about the flour tortillas, feel free to use corn. To each their own.

Ingredients

2 teaspoons olive oil
8 ounces (225 g) mushrooms, thinly sliced (any variety will work: chantrelles, shiitake, button, baby bella, etc.)
½ yellow onion, thinly sliced
Kosher salt and freshly cracked black pepper
Softened butter
4 (8-inch/20-cm) flour tortillas
3 cups (345 g) grated Monterey Jack cheese
Chipotle salsa
Gaby's Famous Guacamole (page 27)
Chopped fresh cilantro

Preheat the oven to 200°F (95°C).

Heat the oil in a large cast-iron skillet over medium-high heat. Add the mushrooms and onion and cook, stirring frequently, until caramelized, 8 to 10 minutes. Season with salt and pepper and remove from the heat. Transfer to a plate and wipe the skillet clean.

Butter one side of each tortilla and place in the skillet buttered side down (still on medium-high heat). Scatter the tortilla with one quarter of the cheese and one quarter of the mushroom mixture. When the tortilla turns just golden brown, 1 to 2 minutes, fold it in half, pressing on it with a spatula to flatten it. Transfer to a baking sheet in the oven to keep warm. Repeat with the remaining ingredients to make three more quesadillas. Serve the folded quesadillas with chipotle salsa, guacamole, and a sprinkling of cilantro.

Serves 4 | Total Time: 20 minutes (Prep: 5. Cook: 15.)

Summer Corn Soup *with* Salsa Verde

Soup is not just for cold weather, which is a good thing to know when you live in a place like California. This version uses sweet summer corn, so it tastes best in the summer when corn is in season (though frozen will also deliver peak freshness) and can be served hot or cold. Serve it as a refreshing accompaniment to grilled meat.

Ingredients

6 cups (870 g) fresh or frozen corn kernels (from about 8 ears of corn)
1 cup (240 ml) water
3 tablespoons unsalted butter
½ sweet onion, diced
2 cups (480 ml) chicken or vegetable broth
Kosher salt and freshly cracked black pepper
½ cup (120 ml) heavy cream
Salsa Verde (page 263)
1 cup (145 g) cherry tomatoes, halved

In a blender, combine 4½ cups (580 g) of the corn kernels and the water and blend until smooth. Work in batches if needed.

In a medium saucepan, melt the butter over medium-high heat. Add the onion and cook until translucent, about 5 minutes. Add the pureed corn, the broth, and 1 cup (145 g) of the remaining corn. Bring to a boil, then reduce the heat and simmer for 8 to 10 minutes, until warmed through. Season with salt and pepper.

Remove from the heat and stir in the cream. Spoon into bowls and serve topped with the remaining corn kernels, a drizzle of salsa verde, and the cherry tomatoes.

Serves 4 | Total Time: 25 minutes (Prep: 10. Cook: 15.)

con su

Grilled Salmon Skewers *with* Basil Vinaigrette

A few years ago, my family and I went on a National Geographic Lindblad Expedition to Alaska. As we cruised along the coast, we were treated to fresh fish every night. While the scenery we took in during the day was pretty magical, it was the fish that I still dream about, especially the salmon. Every year I wait patiently for Copper River salmon season, because this type of salmon is by far the best fish I've ever had. The flesh is the most beautiful red, and it's oh-so-tender, juicy, and flavorful. It's perfect for making these skewers, which get seasoned simply and grilled, letting the fish's natural flavor shine. That said, Copper River salmon has a short season and these skewers will be incredibly tasty with any high-quality salmon you can find. You'll need eight wooden or metal skewers for this recipe (soak wooden skewers in water to cover for about 30 minutes before using).

Ingredients

2 pounds (910 g) salmon, or another fresh fish of your choice
4 lemons
3 tablespoons olive oil
Kosher salt and freshly cracked black pepper
Basil Vinaigrette (page 250)

Preheat an outdoor grill or grill pan to medium-high heat.

Cut the salmon into 1-inch (2.5-cm) cubes and cut 3 of the lemons into very thin slices using a sharp knife or a mandoline.

Alternate threading the salmon and lemon slices on the skewers, using 5 to 6 pieces of salmon per 2 skewers. Drizzle the skewers with oil and season with salt and pepper. Squeeze the juice from half of the remaining lemon on top. Using tongs, carefully transfer the salmon skewers to the grill and grill for about 3 minutes on each side, until the salmon is almost fully cooked through. Remove the salmon skewers from the grill and let rest for about 5 minutes to allow the salmon to finish cooking.

Serve the salmon skewers with the basil vinaigrette and wedges from the remaining lemon half.

Serves 4 | Total Time: 16 minutes (Prep: 10. Cook: 6.)

Grilled Chicken with Summer Succotash

Succotash, or a super-fresh salad made up of summer staples corn and tomatoes, is the perfect side for rich, smoky grilled meat. To keep this meal on the lighter side, I like to stick with chicken, though going with a dark meat by using the thighs delivers way more flavor than the breasts.

Ingredients

¼ cup (60 ml) extra-virgin olive oil
¼ cup (60 ml) fresh lime juice
1 tablespoon ground cumin
1 tablespoon chopped jalapeño chile
1 teaspoon paprika
1 teaspoon garlic salt
½ teaspoon kosher salt
½ teaspoon freshly cracked black pepper
8 boneless, skinless chicken thighs
Summer Succotash (recipe below)

In a medium bowl, combine the oil, lime juice, cumin, chile, paprika, garlic salt, kosher salt, and pepper. Add the chicken thighs, toss to coat, and marinate in the refrigerator for at least 1 hour and up to 8 hours.

Preheat an indoor or outdoor grill to medium-high heat.

Remove the chicken from the marinade. Place it on the grill and cook above direct heat for about 6 to 7 minutes per side, until cooked through. Remove from the grill and transfer to a cutting board to rest for 5 minutes.

Slice the chicken against the grain and serve alongside or on top of the succotash.

Serves 4 | Total Time: At least 1 hour and 30 minutes
(Prep: 15. Cook: 15.)

Summer Succotash

6 ears sweet corn, shucked and cleaned
1 red onion, finely diced
1 red bell pepper, finely diced
1 quart cherry tomatoes, halved
½ cup (20 g) chopped fresh cilantro
½ cup (20 g) chopped fresh basil
¼ cup (13 g) chopped fresh mint
Zest and juice of 1 lime
Kosher salt and freshly cracked black pepper

Preheat an outdoor grill or grill pan to medium-high heat. Place the ears of corn directly on the grill and grill for 10 to 15 minutes, turning every few minutes, until the corn is charred all over. Remove the corn from the grill and let cool completely. Carefully remove the kernels with a knife and transfer the kernels to a serving bowl. Add the red onion, red pepper, cherry tomatoes, cilantro, basil, mint, and lime zest and juice. Season with salt and pepper. Serve at room temperature.

Southwestern Sweet Potato with Quinoa Chili

I can't even begin to tell you how much I love this recipe. I make it in bulk, then freeze it in individual portions so I can have it at a moment's notice. It's a tried-and-true favorite from my blog that I've amped up with even more mix-ins, and it gets topped with whatever chili standbys you love. I'm partial to cheese and avocado because, Hi, have you met me?

Ingredients

For the chili:

1 tablespoon olive oil
1 pound (455 g) ground dark meat turkey (or substitute ground chicken)
Kosher salt and freshly cracked black pepper
1 large red onion, finely chopped
4 cloves garlic, minced
2 tablespoons chili powder
½ teaspoon ground chipotle chile
½ teaspoon ground cumin
3½ cups (840 ml) vegetable stock
1 (14.5-ounce/415-g) can diced tomatoes
1 (15-ounce/425-g) can black beans, drained and rinsed
½ cup (85 g) uncooked quinoa
1 large sweet potato, peeled and cut into ½-inch (12-mm) cubes (about 2 cups/270 g)
1 cup (145 g) frozen corn kernels
Juice of 1 lime, or to taste

For the toppings:

2 avocados, cut into ½-inch (12 mm) cubes
½ cup (20 g) chopped cilantro leaves
½ cup (25 g) sliced scallions, white and light green parts only
Shredded cheddar cheese
Lime wedges

In a large, heavy-bottomed saucepan, heat 1½ teaspoons of the oil. Add the ground turkey, season with salt and pepper, and cook, breaking up the meat with the back of a wooden spoon, until cooked through, about 10 minutes. Remove the meat from the pan to a bowl and set aside.

Heat the remaining 1½ teaspoons oil in the same pan, add the onion, and cook for about 5 minutes, until softened. Season with salt and pepper. Add the garlic, chili powder, chipotle, cumin, and ½ teaspoon salt and stir to combine. Add the stock, tomatoes, black beans, and quinoa and stir to combine. Bring to a boil, then cover, reduce the heat to maintain a gentle simmer, and simmer for 15 minutes. Add the ground turkey, sweet potato, and corn and stir to combine. Return to a simmer and simmer for about 15 minutes more, until the quinoa is fully cooked, the sweet potatoes are softened, and the mixture has thickened into chili. Remove the pan from the heat and add the lime juice. Season with salt if needed. Spoon into bowls and garnish with your choice of toppings: avocado, cilantro, scallions, cheese, and lime wedges.

Serves 6 to 8 | Total Time: 55 minutes (Prep: 10. Cook: 45.)

Veggie Fajita Tacos with Guacamole

I couldn't write a cookbook without talking about Don Antonio's. It's a restaurant within walking distance of my house, and it's our favorite place to go for quick and easy dinner—especially one that involves chips and salsa. Thomas and I go there so much that they don't even give us menus anymore! Thomas always orders the Don Antonio Super Burrito with carne asada and I'm all about the fajitas. I love how the veggies come out sizzling hot with all their smoky charred bits—just begging to be rolled up in a tortilla and heaped with guac. Lucky for those of you who can't just pop in to Don Antonio's, this recipe will deliver that same fajita perfection.

Ingredients

1 tablespoon olive oil
1 poblano pepper, thinly sliced
1 red bell pepper, thinly sliced
1 yellow bell pepper, thinly sliced
½ yellow onion, thinly sliced
½ red onion, thinly sliced
2 cloves garlic, sliced
½ teaspoon kosher salt
½ teaspoon ground cumin
½ teaspoon chili powder
½ teaspoon red pepper flakes
2 tablespoons fresh lime juice, plus more for topping
8 to 12 small flour or corn tortillas, warmed
Gaby's Famous Guacamole (page 27)
½ cup (120 ml) sour cream (optional)
⅓ cup (40 g) crumbed cotija cheese

Heat the oil in a large cast-iron skillet over high heat until smoking. Add the poblano pepper, bell peppers, yellow onion, and red onion and cook until tender and charred, 6 to 8 minutes. During the final minute, add the garlic, salt, cumin, chili powder, red pepper flakes, and lime juice. Remove from the heat and adjust the salt as needed. Stuff into tortillas to make tacos and top with the guacamole, sour cream, cotija cheese, and a squeeze of lime juice.

Serves 4 to 6 | Total Time: 18 minutes (Prep: 10. Cook: 8.)

Blackened **Shrimp Skewers**

These shrimp served alongside a giant salad from Give Me All the Greens! is the ultimate summer dinner. They take no time to make, and yet they're spicy, smoky, and perfect. You'll need eight wooden or metal skewers for this recipe (soak wooden skewers in water for about 30 minutes before using).

Ingredients

Vegetable oil
2 tablespoons ground paprika
1 teaspoon ground cayenne
1 teaspoon garlic powder
1 teaspoon onion powder
2 teaspoons kosher salt
1 teaspoon freshly cracked black pepper
½ teaspoon dried thyme
½ teaspoon dried basil
½ teaspoon dried oregano
2 pounds (910 g) shrimp (26 to 30 count), peeled and deveined
1 bunch scallions, white and light green parts, cut into 2-inch (5-cm) pieces
3 lemons, cut in half

Preheat an outdoor grill or grill pan over medium-high heat and lightly oil it.

In a small bowl, combine the paprika, cayenne, garlic powder, onion powder, salt, pepper, thyme, basil, and oregano.

Season both sides of the shrimp liberally with the spice mixture to fully cover them. Thread the seasoned shrimp on metal or soaked wooden skewers, alternating each shrimp with a piece of scallion, using about 6 shrimp per skewer to make 8 skewers.

Place the halved lemons on the grill and grill for about 2 minutes, until grill marks appear. This helps the lemons get extra juicy and brings out even more flavor. Remove once charred and set aside.

Lay the shrimp skewers on the grill or grill pan and grill, flipping once, until the shrimp are pink and opaque, 5 to 6 minutes total. Remove from the grill and serve with the charred lemon halves.

Serves 4 to 6 | Total Time: 18 minutes (Prep: 10. Cook: 8.)

Fish Tacos *with* Pineapple-Mango Salsa

Everyone always says that fish tacos are the quintessential California recipe, so here you go: The Most Amazing Fish Tacos on the Whole Planet (in my not-so-humble opinion). What's the key to perfect fish tacos? 1) Perfectly crispy fish. 2) Salsa. 3) Slaw (and no, this isn't a mayo-based slaw, thank you very much). 4) Chipotle crema. You can thank me later.

Ingredients

For the cabbage slaw:

1 cup (95 g) finely shredded green cabbage
1 cup (95 g) finely shredded red cabbage
½ yellow onion, thinly sliced
¼ cup (60 ml) apple cider vinegar or red wine vinegar
2 tablespoons water
½ teaspoon kosher salt
½ teaspoon brown sugar
½ teaspoon dried oregano
½ teaspoon red pepper flakes

For the fish:

2 pounds (910 g) cod fillets
Olive oil
½ teaspoon ground cumin
Kosher salt and freshly cracked black pepper
1 lime

For assembly:

1 to 2 teaspoons adobo sauce from a can of chipotle chiles
½ cup (120 ml) sour cream
8 corn tortillas, warmed
Pineapple-Mango Salsa (page 255)

To make the cabbage slaw: In a large bowl, combine the cabbages and onion. In a separate bowl, combine the vinegar, water, salt, brown sugar, oregano, and red pepper flakes. Pour the vinegar mixture over the cabbage mixture and stir to coat. Cover and refrigerate for at least 2 hours, and up to 8 hours, before serving.

To make the fish: Preheat an outdoor grill or grill pan over medium-high heat.

Drizzle the cod with a touch of oil, add the cumin, and season with salt and pepper. Grill for 5 to 6 minutes on each side, until the fish flakes easily, is cooked through, and has a golden-brown crust. Remove the fish from the grill and squeeze the juice from the lime over it. Adjust the salt and pepper as needed.

To assemble: In a small bowl, whisk the adobo sauce into the sour cream. Place a few large pieces of the flaked fish into a warmed tortilla. Top with a spoonful of the pineapple-mango salsa, 1 tablespoon of the adobo sour cream, and 2 tablespoons of the cabbage slaw. Repeat with the remaining tortillas and filling and serve immediately.

Serves 4 to 6 | Total Time: At least 2 hours and 20 minutes (Prep: 10. Cook: 10 to 12.)

Taco *Skillet* Bake

This is the ultimate Mama Dalkin recipe, and making it always brings me back to the good old days when I lived at home and got to eat her delicious food every night. It's tacos meets casserole bake, and when you make it, you can feel the love. It's not hard to believe that all this gooey, cheesy, spicy goodness is a real crowd-pleaser, too.

Ingredients

1 tablespoon olive oil
1 yellow onion, chopped
1 red bell pepper, chopped
1 poblano pepper, chopped
1½ pounds (680 g) ground turkey or chicken (preferably dark meat)
2 tablespoons chili powder
1 teaspoon kosher salt
½ teaspoon garlic powder
½ teaspoon onion powder
½ teaspoon dried oregano
½ teaspoon ground cumin
½ teaspoon red pepper flakes
½ teaspoon paprika
¼ teaspoon ground cayenne
1 (14.5-ounce/415-g) can fire-roasted tomatoes with chiles
1 cup (145 g) frozen corn kernels
½ cup (90 g) cooked black beans
1½ cups (170 g) Mexican-blend shredded cheese

Garnishes:

1 ripe avocado, pitted, peeled, and diced
5 scallions, white and light green parts, sliced on the diagonal
3 to 4 tablespoons chopped fresh cilantro
Tortilla chips

In a large cast-iron skillet, heat the oil over medium-high heat. Add the onion, red pepper, and poblano pepper and cook for 5 minutes, or until softened. Add the ground turkey and cook, breaking it apart with the back of a wooden spoon, until no pink remains, about 10 minutes. Add the chili powder, salt, garlic powder, onion powder, oregano, cumin, red pepper flakes, paprika, and cayenne and stir to combine. Add the fire-roasted tomatoes, corn, and black beans. Bring to a simmer, then reduce the heat to low and simmer for 10 minutes until the liquid has slightly reduced.

Sprinkle the cheese over the top of the skillet, cover, then turn the heat off and leave for a few minutes for the cheese to melt from the residual heat. Serve right from the skillet with a garnish of avocado, scallions, and cilantro with tortilla chips alongside.

Serves 4 to 6 | Total Time: 35 minutes (Prep: 10. Cook: 25.)

Chapter 7:

Weekend Par-tays

This girl—me—LOVES to entertain. I first got inspired when I was working as a private chef for one of the chicest moms in Malibu, Simone, who threw the most incredible parties. Every Sunday she'd host a huge family dinner and invite everyone in the neighborhood for a cook-out. We'd make enough food to feed a small village, and everyone would drink rosé and hang out until it was time to put the kids to bed. I loved how relaxed everyone was and that nothing felt overly fussed. She taught me how, with a little advance planning and smart menu choices, hosting doesn't have to be stressful. Now one of my favorite things in the world is having people over, for any occasion or for no reason at all. And these are my favorite recipes for ensuring a great time.

Dad's BBQ Chicken

Bruce, aka my dad, makes the best chicken in the whole wide world. He's probably going to be mad that I called him Bruce, but Bruce is quite possibly the coolest name ever, am I right? Anyway, Dad nails it with the BBQ chicken. It's an art form, and no one is allowed to mess with the chicken while he's doing his thing. According to him, the basting is key because it locks in all the flavor. I suggest serving it with salsa verde because while I used to love dipping the chicken into ketchup, that look just isn't as cute on a thirty-year-old.

Ingredients

For the BBQ chicken:

1½ tablespoons paprika
1½ tablespoons garlic powder
1 teaspoon kosher salt
1 teaspoon freshly cracked black pepper
2 whole chickens, cleaned and giblets removed
Vegetable oil, for the grill

For the BBQ chicken baste:

3 tablespoons melted unsalted butter
½ teaspoon paprika
½ teaspoon garlic salt
¼ teaspoon kosher salt
¼ teaspoon freshly cracked black pepper

For serving:

Salsa Verde (page 263)

Preheat a gas or charcoal grill over high heat for indirect grilling.

To make the BBQ chicken: In a small bowl, stir together the paprika, garlic powder, salt, and pepper and season the chickens inside and out with the mixture. Let stand while the grill heats.

To make the BBQ chicken baste: Combine the melted butter and the BBQ chicken baste seasonings in a bowl and whisk to combine.

Lightly oil the grill rack. Place the chickens directly on the grill over indirect heat, breast side up to start, and cover the grill. Grill for 30 minutes, then flip the chicken over and grill for 15 minutes more. Using a basting brush, baste the chicken with the BBQ chicken baste and grill for another 15 minutes. Flip the chicken again, baste, and continue grilling for 15 minutes more (1 hour and 15 minutes total), or until an instant-read thermometer inserted into the thickest part of a thigh, away from the bone, registers 170°F (77°C).

To serve: Transfer the chickens to a carving board and let rest for 10 to 15 minutes. Carve the chickens and serve immediately with the salsa verde.

Serves 6 to 8 | Total Time: About 1 hour and 40 minutes
(Prep: 10. Cook: 1 hour and 15 minutes.)

Garlic Chimichurri Mussels

When I'm working on a new recipe, I'll crowdsource on Snapchat to see what people are into. When I asked everyone whether they preferred clams or mussels, the overwhelming response was mussels, so I'm giving the people what they want! (That said, you could totally make this recipe with clams.) There's really nothing like a big pot of steaming-hot mussels soaking in an herb-infused broth, and making a big batch for a crowd is super-quick and easy. You can put the pot right on the table and serve with a loaf of good crusty bread and plenty of white wine or bubbles.

Ingredients

2 tablespoons olive oil
6 cloves garlic, finely chopped
2 shallots, white and light green parts, finely chopped
1 red Fresno chile, thinly sliced
1 cup (240 ml) dry white wine
4 to 5 pounds (1.8 to 2.2 kg) mussels, scrubbed and rinsed clean
2 tablespoons roughly chopped fresh parsley
2 tablespoons roughly chopped fresh cilantro
1 tablespoon roughly chopped fresh oregano
1 tablespoon red wine vinegar
Grilled or toasted baguette

Heat the oil in a large, shallow skillet over medium heat. Add the garlic, shallots, and chile and cook for 2 minutes, or until the garlic is fragrant, taking care that the garlic doesn't burn. Add the wine, increase the heat to medium-high, and bring to a simmer.

Add the mussels, cover, and cook for 6 to 8 minutes, stirring occasionally, until the mussels have opened. Discard any mussels that are still closed. Add the parsley, cilantro, oregano, and vinegar and give the pot a quick stir.

Transfer the mussels and their cooking liquid to a large serving bowl and serve with pieces of toasted bread to soak up the juices.

Serves 4 | Total Time: 20 minutes (Prep: 10. Cook: 10.)

Charred Octopus Tacos

I know what you're thinking (octopus?!), *but trust me on this one. When you cook it in a flavorful broth until it's perfectly tender, toss it with smoky paprika and cumin, and give it a good char on the grill, it ranks right up there with the best taco fillers.*

Ingredients

1 cup (125 g) finely diced white onion
⅓ cup (15 g) chopped fresh cilantro
1 yellow onion, cut in half
1 head garlic, cut in half
2 bay leaves
1 teaspoon kosher salt
1 teaspoon black peppercorns
3 quarts water
3 pounds (1.3 kg) octopus (½ to ¾ pound/225 to 340 g each), cleaned and beaks removed
2 tablespoons olive oil
2 teaspoons smoked paprika
½ teaspoon ground cumin
Kosher salt and freshly cracked black pepper
12 small flour or corn tortillas
3 ripe avocados, pitted, peeled, and quartered
Tomatillo-Avocado Salsa (page 256)

In a small bowl, combine the white onion and cilantro and set aside.

In a large Dutch oven, combine the yellow onion, garlic, bay leaves, salt, peppercorns, and water and bring to a boil. Add the octopus to the liquid and bring it back to a boil, then reduce the heat to maintain a simmer and simmer for 90 minutes, or until tender. Turn off the heat and let the octopus cool in the liquid for 30 minutes.

Remove the octopus from the liquid. Using a paper towel, scrape off any excess skin from the octopus. Transfer the octopus to a medium bowl and toss with the oil, paprika, and cumin and season with salt and pepper.

Preheat an outdoor grill or grill pan to medium-high heat.

Transfer the octopus to the grill and grill until lightly charred on the bottom, about 2 minutes. Flip and continue to char on the second side for 2 to 3 minutes more. Remove from the grill, transfer to a cutting board, and cut the octopus into individual tentacles.

Heat the tortillas over an open flame. Smash an avocado quarter on the bottom of each tortilla. Top with the charred octopus, sprinkle with the white onion and cilantro mixture, and finish with the tomatillo-avocado salsa. Fold into tacos and serve immediately.

Serves 4 to 6 | Total Time: 2 hours and 20 minutes
(Prep: 15. Cook: 1 hour and 35 minutes.)

Heirloom Cherry Tomato Tart

This is the perfect recipe to have in your back pocket when you're having a vegetarian over for dinner (or lunch or brunch)—or when you just want something super-tasty that doesn't involve meat. It has a pine nut crust that gets topped with homemade ricotta cheese (such an impressive crowd-pleaser that's so completely easy) and studded with cherry tomatoes. It's as delicious as it is gorgeous. Slice it up and serve with a salad alongside.

Ingredients

For the dough:

3 tablespoons toasted pine nuts
1¼ cups (155 g) all-purpose flour, plus more for rolling
Pinch of kosher salt
½ cup (1 stick/155 g) European-style unsalted butter
2 to 4 tablespoons (30 to 60 ml) ice-cold water

For the filling:

1 cup (245 g) fresh ricotta cheese (page 38)
4 ounces (115 g) cream cheese, at room temperature
½ cup (50 g) grated pecorino romano cheese, plus more for garnish
1 teaspoon lemon zest
1 teaspoon fresh lemon juice
1 tablespoon chopped fresh basil
1 teaspoon chopped fresh oregano
Kosher salt and freshly cracked black pepper

To make the dough: Place the pine nuts in a spice grinder and grind until pulverized.

In a large bowl, combine the flour, ground pine nuts, and salt. With your hands, cut the cold butter into the flour mixture, leaving some pea-size pieces of butter. Add the cold water starting with 2 tablespoons, stirring with a wooden spoon and gradually adding as much water as you need to bring the dough together without making it too moist. Turn the dough out onto a piece of plastic wrap, shape it into a disk, wrap it up, and refrigerate for 30 minutes to 1 hour.

To make the filling: In a medium bowl, mix together the ricotta cheese, cream cheese, and pecorino with a rubber spatula, blending well. Fold in the lemon zest, lemon juice, basil, and oregano and season with salt and pepper. Set aside.

Preheat the oven to 400°F (205°C).

To assemble the tart: Remove the dough from the refrigerator and place it on a lightly floured work surface. With a floured rolling pin, roll the dough into a 12-inch (30.5-cm) circle. Place the dough into a 10-inch (25-cm) nonstick tart pan with a removable bottom, trimming the sides to a ½-inch (12-mm) overhang. Fold in the excess dough and pinch into the sides of the tart. Prick the bottom of the tart all over with a fork. Place the tart pan in the freezer for 15 minutes.

(ingredients and recipe continue)

For the topping:

- 3 cups (435 g) heirloom cherry tomatoes, halved or quartered if large
- ½ shallot, thinly sliced
- 1 tablespoon extra-virgin olive oil
- 2 teaspoons balsamic vinegar
- Kosher salt and freshly cracked black pepper

For the garnishes:

- 2 tablespoons toasted pine nuts
- Handful of microgreens
- ½ cup (20 g) fresh torn basil
- ½ cup (20 g) oregano leaves
- Kosher salt and freshly cracked black pepper

Remove the tart pan from the freezer and place it on a baking sheet. Line the tart shell with parchment paper or foil and fill with dried beans or baking weights. Place in the oven and bake for 15 minutes, then remove the parchment and beans and bake for another 20 to 25 minutes, until golden brown. Remove from the oven and cool in the pan on a wire rack for 15 to 20 minutes.

To make the topping: In a large bowl, toss the tomatoes and shallots with the oil and vinegar. Season with salt and pepper.

Remove the tart from the pan and place it on a serving plate. Fill with the cheese mixture and top with the tomato topping.

To garnish: Sprinkle with the toasted pine nuts, microgreens, basil, oregano, a sprinkle of salt and pepper, and a dusting of pecorino cheese.

Serves 6 to 8 | Total Time: About 2 hours
(Prep: 20. Cook: 35 to 40.)

Double-Double Gaby-Style Burger

Every time we drive to Palm Springs from LA, it's non-negotiable that we stop at In-N-Out Burger for road-trip snacks. Since we can't go to Palm Springs every weekend (such a bummer), I needed to find another way to get a fix. This recipe is for my favorite version of this classic California burger: two beef patties (heck yeah!), no mustard, tons of homemade chipotle ketchup, and a lettuce wrap instead of a bun (I love the crispness and it also helps save a few calories).

Ingredients

2 tablespoons olive oil
2 yellow onions, finely diced
½ cup (120 ml) water
Kosher salt
2 pounds (910 g) 80% fat ground beef
Freshly cracked black pepper
2 tablespoons unsalted butter
8 slices habanero Jack cheese (or gouda, havarti, cheddar, or American)
8 butter lettuce or iceberg lettuce leaves
8 tomato slices
Homemade Chipotle Ketchup (page 259)

In a large skillet, heat the oil over medium-high heat. Add the onions and cook for 10 to 15 minutes, until they start to caramelize. Reduce the heat to medium, add the water, and continue to caramelize for another 30 minutes, or until deeply browned but not burnt. Season with salt and set aside.

In a large bowl, season the ground beef with plenty of salt and pepper and mix to combine. Divide the mixture into 8 portions and form them into very thin patties.

Heat a griddle over high heat. Add 1 tablespoon of the butter to the griddle and swirl it around to evenly coat. Place 4 patties on the griddle and cook for 3 to 4 minutes on the first side. Flip and cook for an additional 2 minutes. Top with a slice of cheese and leave for about 1 minute to melt. Repeat with the remaining butter, patties, and cheese.

Place one patty on top of another and place the double patty on a lettuce leaf. Top with caramelized onions, tomato slices, and chipotle ketchup and wrap with a second lettuce leaf. Repeat to make three more burgers. Serve immediately.

Serves 4 | Total Time: 1 hour (Prep: 5. Cook: 55.)

K-Town Melt-in-Your-Mouth Baby Back Ribs

My friend Adam makes the most incredible ribs that are the perfect sweet-spicy mash-up—almost exactly like the ones I love to order in Koreatown, complete with spicy pickles (OMG wait until you guys try these pickle—game changers). I bribed him to get the recipe for this book, and he very generously agreed, which means that you can put out a platter at your next game night/pool party/ Sunday football viewing. Just be sure to have napkins handy, because there's no other way to eat these than getting down and dirty.

Ingredients

For the spicy pickles:

1 pound (455 g) Persian cucumbers, sliced ½ inch (12 mm) thick
1 rounded tablespoon kosher salt
2 to 4 cloves garlic, thinly sliced or minced
1 tablespoon grated fresh ginger
6 scallions, white and light green parts, chopped
5 tablespoons rice vinegar
1 jalapeño chile, thinly sliced, seeds removed for less heat
1 tablespoon honey
1 teaspoon low-sodium soy sauce
½ teaspoon toasted sesame oil

For the ribs:

2 tablespoons sugar
1 tablespoon kosher salt
½ teaspoon ground ginger
1 tablespoon chili powder
2 racks baby back ribs
1 cup (240 ml) water or beer

For the Korean BBQ sauce:

½ cup (120 ml) gochujang (Korean chile paste)
1 teaspoon chili powder
8 to 10 cloves garlic, minced
½ jalapeño chile, minced

To make the spicy pickles: Place the cucumbers in a colander set over a bowl, sprinkle with the salt, and give them a quick toss to evenly coat them in the salt. Let sit for 30 minutes. Rinse the salt off the cucumbers and pat dry.

In a large bowl, combine the cucumbers, garlic, ginger, scallions, vinegar, chile, honey, soy sauce, and sesame oil and stir to coat. Cover and refrigerate for at least 4 hours or overnight.

To make the ribs: In a small bowl, combine the sugar, salt, ginger, and chili powder. Place the ribs on a baking sheet and rub the spice mixture all over ribs, top and bottom. Cover with foil and place in the refrigerator for 4 hours or, even better, overnight.

Preheat the oven to 350°F (175°C).

Remove the ribs from the refrigerator and peel back a corner of the foil. Pour in the water or beer, close up the foil, and place the ribs in the oven. Bake for 2 hours, or until the meat nearly falls off the bone.

To make the Korean BBQ sauce: In a medium bowl, combine all the sauce ingredients. (The sauce can be made in advance and stored in the refrigerator.)

Remove the ribs from the oven and fire up the grill to medium-high heat. Liberally brush the ribs with the BBQ sauce, place the ribs on the grill, and grill for 7 to 8 minutes on each side, until charred. Remove from the grill and add more sauce if you like.

(ingredients and recipe continue)

¼ cup (50 g) peeled and minced ginger
5 tablespoons (75 ml) low-sodium soy sauce
2 tablespoons rice vinegar
2 tablespoons light brown sugar
2 tablespoons honey
1 tablespoon toasted sesame oil

For the toppings:
4 scallions, white and light green parts, chopped
2 tablespoons toasted sesame seeds
1 jalapeño chile, thinly sliced

To top and serve: Slice the racks into individual ribs and toss in more BBQ sauce. Arrange on a platter and top with the chopped scallions, sesame seeds, jalapeño, and spicy pickles.

Serves 6 to 8 | Total Time: 6 hours and 30 minutes to 12 hours (Prep: 15. Cook: 2 hours and 15 minutes.)

Cioppino *with Grilled* Garlic Sourdough

I went to college right outside of San Francisco, and one of my favorite food memories is cioppino, a fisherman's stew that's native to the Bay Area and includes a mishmash of ingredients from the sea along with white wine, tomatoes, and plenty of garlic and basil. My friends and I would go into the city on weekends just to have it for lunch, and it would come out with freshly made sourdough for dipping. I still love whipping up a big bowlful for company, with my added simple twist of grilling the bread.

Ingredients

¼ cup (60 ml) olive oil
½ teaspoon red pepper flakes
1 large yellow onion, finely diced
1 leek, white and light green parts only, cleaned and thinly sliced into half moons
1 red bell pepper, finely diced
6 cloves garlic, minced
Kosher salt
2 cups (480 ml) white wine
2 (28-ounce/840-ml) cans crushed tomatoes
2 cups (480 ml) fish stock
10 to 12 fresh basil leaves
1 pound (455 g) littleneck clams, scrubbed cleaned
1 pound (455 g) mussels, scrubbed clean and beards removed right before cooking
1 pound (455 g) large shrimp (26 to 30 count), peeled and deveined
2 pounds (910 g) halibut or sea bass, cut roughly into 2-inch (5-cm) cubes
1 to 2 pounds (455 to 910 g) cooked crab (or packaged lump crabmeat)
½ cup (25 g) chopped fresh flat-leaf parsley
Freshly cracked black pepper
Grilled garlic sourdough bread

In a large Dutch oven, heat the oil over medium-high heat. Add the red pepper flakes. Add the onion, leek, and red pepper and cook for 10 to 12 minutes, until softened. Add the garlic and cook for 30 seconds. Stir in 1 teaspoon salt. Pour in the wine and let the alcohol cook out for 2 to 3 minutes, then add the crushed tomatoes, fish stock, and basil. Bring to a boil, then reduce the heat to maintain a simmer and simmer for 20 minutes.

Add the clams and mussels to the broth, making sure to tuck them into the liquid. After about 5 to 6 minutes, they'll start to open, then add the shrimp and sea bass and cook for 4 to 5 minutes, until both are cooked through—the shrimp should be pink and the fish should flake easily when poked. Stir in the crab and let it warm up. Add the parsley, taste the broth, and season with salt and pepper as needed. Serve immediately with a side of grilled garlic sourdough.

Serves 4 to 6 | Total Time: 50 to 55 minutes
(Prep: 10. Cook: 40 to 45.)

Grilled Sourdough

Heat a grill or grill pan over medium-hight heat. Drizzle both sides of a piece of bread with olive oil. Transfer to the grill and grill for 2 to 3 minutes until grill marks appear. Flip with a pair of tongs and repeat. Remove from grill, gently rub a garlic clove over both sides of the bread, and serve as needed.

Carnitas and Black Bean Nachos with Charred Corn Salsa

I feel about nachos the same way Thomas feels about breakfast burritos: there's an art form to them that we must obey. There has to be plenty of cheese on each chip, some kind of protein, even more cheese by way of queso, and plenty of fixins on top—corn salsa, guacamole, black beans, scallions, just to name a few. Assemble these on a sheet tray or in a large baking dish and let your guests demolish them straight out of the oven.

Ingredients

For the carnitas:

2 pounds (910 g) boneless pork shoulder, cut into 2-inch (5-cm) cubes
½ cup (120 ml) fresh orange juice
¼ cup (60 ml) fresh lime juice
1¼ cups (300 ml) chipotle salsa
1 teaspoon kosher salt, or to taste

For the queso:

1 tablespoon unsalted butter
1 clove garlic, chopped
1 tablespoon all-purpose flour
½ cup (120 ml) milk
4 ounces (115 g) freshly grated Monterey Jack cheese
Kosher salt and freshly cracked black pepper

For serving:

1 (16-ounce/455 g) bag tortilla chips
16 ounces (450 g) freshly grated Monterey Jack cheese
1 cup (185 g) cooked black beans, rinsed and drained
Charred Corn Salsa (page 254)
½ cup (25 g) chopped scallions
½ cup (20 g) chopped fresh cilantro
1 jalapeño chile, thinly sliced
Gaby's Famous Guacamole (page 27)

To make the carnitas: Place the pork in a large Dutch oven and add the orange juice, lime juice, salsa, and salt. Add enough water to barely cover the meat. Place over medium-high heat and bring to a boil. Cover, reduce the heat to medium-low, and simmer for 2 hours, or until the pork is falling apart to the touch. Uncover the pot, increase the heat to medium-high, and cook the pork for about another 45 minutes, stirring occasionally, until all the liquid has evaporated, the pork fat is rendered, and most of the pork is golden brown. Remove the pot from the stove and adjust the seasoning as needed.

Preheat the oven to 350°F (175°C).

To make the queso: Melt the butter in a small saucepan over medium heat. Add in the garlic, then stir in the flour and cook for 1 to 2 minutes, stirring often, until a golden roux is formed. While stirring, slowly add the milk. Cook, stirring frequently, for 5 minutes, until it thickens slightly. Add the grated cheese, stirring until melted. Season with salt and pepper.

To serve: Layer half of the tortilla chips on a large baking sheet and top them with half of the carnitas, half of the grated cheese, and half of the beans. Add another layer of chips, carnitas, cheese, and beans. Transfer the baking sheet to the oven and bake for 5 to 10 minutes, until the cheese is melted. Remove from the oven and drizzle with the queso, then top with the corn salsa, scallions, cilantro, and jalapeño and serve with guacamole alongside.

Serves 6 to 8 | Total Time: 3 hours and 10 minutes
(Prep: 15. Cook: 2 hours and 55 minutes.)

Whole-Roasted Branzino with Shaved-Fennel Slaw

I totally subscribe to the fake-it-til-you-make-it way of thinking, so when I cooked a party for one of my girlfriends, Geri, and she requested whole-roasted fish, even though I'd never made it before I said "sure!" Luckily, it's super-easy and the payoff is huge. The fish should already be cleaned (read: gutted) thanks to your fishmonger, so all you need to do is stuff it with citrus, fennel, salt, and pepper and roast until its meat is juicy, flaky, and perfectly done. It makes for a beautiful and impressive presentation too, especially topped with a pretty fennel slaw.

Ingredients

For the fennel slaw:

1 large fennel bulb (or 2 medium bulbs)
Juice of 1 lemon
1 tablespoon champagne vinegar
2 cloves garlic, finely chopped
1 shallot, finely chopped
⅓ cup (75 ml) olive oil
Kosher salt and freshly cracked black pepper
10 fresh mint leaves, torn into pieces

For the branzini:

4 tablespoons (60 ml) olive oil
2 (1-pound/455-g) whole branzini, scaled, gutted, and cleaned
Kosher salt and freshly cracked black pepper
1 lemon, very thinly sliced
½ orange, very thinly sliced
4 sprigs fresh flat-leaf parsley
1 lemon, cut into wedges

To make the fennel slaw: Carefully pick off the fennel fronds and set them aside. Using a mandoline, shave the fennel bulb into ⅛-inch (3-mm) slices.

In a medium bowl, whisk together the lemon juice, vinegar, garlic, shallot, and oil. Season with salt and pepper and add the mint. Toss all but a few pieces of the shaved fennel and almost all of the fennel fronds with the vinaigrette and let sit for 1 hour.

To make the branzini: Preheat the oven to 450°F (230°C). Spread 2 tablespoons of the oil over a large rimmed baking sheet to fully coat it.

Rinse the branzini well and pat dry with paper towels. Place the fish on the prepared baking sheet. Season the cavity and exterior of each fish with salt and pepper. Alternating slices of the citrus, stuff the cavity with 2 lemon slices, 2 orange slices, and a few slices of the reserved fennel and fennel fronds. Place a few slices of lemon over the top of each fish. Drizzle with the remaining 2 tablespoons oil and roast until cooked through, about 15 minutes.

Turn the oven to broil and broil for 2 minutes, just to give it an extra hint of golden color.

Transfer the fish to a serving platter and serve topped with the fennel slaw and the lemon wedges alongside.

Serves 4 | Total Time: 1 hour and 30 minutes
(Prep: 10. Cook: 17 to 20.)

Perfect Meatballs *with* Cherry Tomato Sauce

I always hear from people that they're on the hunt for the perfect meatball recipe because the ones they make are too bready, too beefy, or too dense with just meat. Well, your search ends here. The key is tossing a combination of beef and pork with panko bread crumbs, which gives the meatballs the perfect texture and balance of flavor. (I've been known to forget the pork from time to time; ground turkey is a great substitute.) They freeze well, so it's easy to make a big batch and just reheat when you have people coming over for dinner—smothered with a quick cherry tomato sauce and cheese, of course. And if you need an excuse to make extra, I strongly encourage you to use the leftovers for Adam's Meatball Subs (page 207).

Ingredients

For the meatballs:

1 pound (455 g) ground beef sirloin
1 pound (455 g) ground pork
1½ cups (120 g) panko bread crumbs
¼ cup (60 ml) milk
4 large eggs
1 cup (50 g) chopped fresh flat-leaf parsley
1 cup (40 g) torn fresh basil, plus more for garnish
4 cloves garlic, finely chopped
1 teaspoon kosher salt
½ teaspoon freshly cracked black pepper
½ teaspoon red pepper flakes
¼ cup (60 ml) extra-virgin olive oil, plus 2 tablespoons extra for cooking
½ cup (50 g) freshly grated Parmesan cheese
⅓ cup (45 g) pine nuts

For the cherry tomato sauce:

2 tablespoons unsalted butter
1 tablespoon olive oil
1 shallot, finely chopped

Preheat the oven to 350°F (175°C).

To make the meatballs: In a large bowl, combine the beef, pork, ½ cup (40 g) of the panko, the milk, and eggs and set aside. In a food processor, combine the parsley, basil, garlic, salt, pepper, red pepper flakes, oil, Parmesan, and pine nuts. Process for 30 to 45 seconds, until the herbs are finely chopped. Add the herb mixture to the meat mixture and mix until the ingredients are incorporated. Shape the meatballs into large balls, bigger than a golf ball and smaller than a tennis ball (to make about 18 meatballs), then roll them in the remaining 1 cup (80 g) panko.

In a large skillet, heat the remaining 2 tablespoons of olive oil over medium-high heat. Add the meatballs and cook to seal the crust, then flip them over and cook until crispy on all sides, 8 minutes total. Transfer to a 9 by 13-inch (23 by 33-cm) baking dish, and wipe down the skillet.

To make the cherry tomato sauce: In the same pan, melt the butter with the oil over medium-high heat. Add the shallot, garlic, and red pepper flakes and cook until fragrant, about 2 minutes. Add the cherry tomatoes and cook until they start to fall apart, 7 to 8 minutes. Add the crushed tomatoes and season with salt and pepper. Bring to a simmer, then reduce the heat and simmer until reduced slightly, about 10 minutes.

(ingredients and recipe continue)

3 cloves garlic, roughly chopped
½ teaspoon red pepper flakes
1½ pounds (680 g) cherry tomatoes, halved
14 ounces (420 ml) canned crushed tomatoes
Kosher salt and freshly cracked black pepper

For serving:
8 ounces (225 g) fresh mozzarella, sliced
Fresh basil leaves
Basil Vinaigrette (page 250)
Cooked pasta or polenta for serving

To serve: Pour the tomato mixture over the meatballs and top with the mozzarella. Bake for 25 to 30 minutes until the cheese has melted and is bubbly. Garnish with basil, drizzle with basil vinaigrette, and serve over pasta (or with polenta) on the side.

Serves 8+ | Total Time: 1 hour and 10 minutes
(Prep: 10. Cook: 1 hour.)

Your Go-to **Risotto** with All the Variations

I hear from people quite frequently that they are FREAKED OUT by risotto because it seems super-fancy and super-hard to make. Yes, you have to babysit the pot while it's cooking, but the reality is that it's an easy dish to make (it's essentially all stirring) and also to riff on with tons of variations. Below is my base recipe that's delicious on its own, or you can add any of the toppings and mix-ins that I've listed here.

Ingredients

2 tablespoons unsalted butter
1 shallot, finely chopped
1 clove garlic, finely chopped
1 cup (190 g) Arborio rice
½ cup (120 ml) dry white wine
3 cups (720 ml) chicken or vegetable stock
⅓ cup (30 g) grated Parmesan cheese
2 tablespoons mascarpone cheese
Kosher salt and freshly cracked black pepper
Fresh lemon juice

In a large skillet, melt the butter over medium-high heat. Add the shallot and garlic and cook for 1 minute, or until fragrant. Add the rice and stir for 1 minute to toast it.

Add the wine and stir to combine. Cook until all the wine has been absorbed, about 3 minutes, and then start adding the chicken stock ½ cup (120 ml) at a time, letting each addition absorb before adding the next. Continue to cook, stirring every minute or so, for 25 to 30 minutes, until all of the stock has been added and the rice is tender but still al dente. Remove from the heat and stir in the Parmesan and mascarpone cheeses. Season with salt and pepper and squeeze in some lemon juice. Serve immediately, with any toppings you like. Here are a few ideas:

- Sautéed mushrooms (page 116)
- Charred corn
- Grilled shrimp
- Blanched peas
- Roasted butternut squash
- Roasted asparagus (page 124)
- Crispy pancetta

Serves 4 | Total Time: 40 minutes (Prep: 5. Cook: 35.)

Balsamic Grilled Flank Steak with Charred Tomatoes

This is the dish that everyone should have in his or her summer entertaining rotation. Flank steak is made for the grill and it has great, rich flavor that you can bring out even more with a balsamic marinade. Serve it with some charred tomatoes over the top and a drizzle of basil vinaigrette and you have the perfect backyard meal.

Ingredients

For the steak:

⅔ cup (165 ml) olive oil
½ cup (120 ml) balsamic vinegar
4 cloves garlic, finely chopped
Kosher salt and freshly cracked black pepper
5 to 6 sprigs thyme
1 (3-pound/1.3-kg) piece flank steak (or skirt steak)

For the charred tomatoes:

1 tablespoon olive oil
1 shallot, thinly sliced
3 cloves garlic, sliced
1 pint (290 g) heirloom cherry tomatoes
Kosher salt and freshly cracked black pepper

For serving:

Basil Vinaigrette (page 250)

To make the steak: In a large nonreactive bowl, whisk together the oil, vinegar, and garlic and season with salt and pepper. Add the thyme. Add the meat to the bowl and flip it to coat. Cover with plastic wrap and refrigerate for at least 8 hours and up to 24 hours.

To make the charred tomatoes: Heat the oil in your heaviest cast-iron skillet over medium-high heat. Add the shallot and garlic and cook for 1 minute, or until fragrant. Add the cherry tomatoes and cook without stirring for 2 minutes, or until they start to blister. Give them a quick stir, turn off the heat, and let them sit for another 2 minutes or so. Season with salt and pepper.

Preheat an outdoor grill or grill pan to medium-high heat and oil the grates. Remove the steak from the marinade, letting excess drip off. Season liberally with salt and pepper. Grill the steak, turning occasionally, until lightly charred all over, 10 to 12 minutes for medium. Transfer the steak to a cutting board and let rest for 5 to 10 minutes.

To serve: Thinly slice the meat against the grain and serve with the basil vinaigrette and charred tomatoes on top.

Serves 6 to 8 | Total Time: At least 8 hours and 20 minutes (Prep: 5. Cook: 15.)

Santa Maria Tri-Tip with Salsa and Guacamole

As I mentioned at the beginning of this chapter, one of my private chef clients loved to entertain, and before I came into the picture she would usually just grab a few premade tri-tip steaks and put them out with salsa and guacamole. I, of course, wanted to take this to the next level, but I also wanted to honor the spirit of the dish. After all, tri-tip is classic California—it's a popular triangular-shaped, super-marbled cut that's most often used for our style of barbecue, which is less low and slow and more quick and dirty on the grill. It's super-tender and doesn't need a lot of extra love to get it where you want it to go, just a simple rub and fire. Traditionally tri-tip is barbecued over cherry oak chips and briquettes, but a gas grill will do the trick. Then it's sliced up and served alongside salsa and guacamole.

Ingredients

For the spice rub:

2 tablespoons finely ground coffee
1½ tablespoons kosher salt
1½ tablespoons garlic powder
1 teaspoon freshly cracked black pepper
1 tablespoon brown sugar
½ teaspoon dried oregano
¼ teaspoon dried thyme
¼ teaspoon paprika
¼ teaspoon ground cayenne

1 whole tri-tip (about 2 pounds/910 g)
Small 6-inch (15-cm) tortillas
Chipotle salsa
Gaby's Famous Guacamole (page 27)

To make the rub: In a small bowl, whisk together the rub ingredients. Trim the silver skin off the tri-tip but leave some of the fat. Massage the meat with the rub until fully covered. Place on a plate and let rest at room temperature for 1 hour.

Preheat an outdoor grill or grill pan to high heat.

Place the tri-tip on the grill and sear well on one side, 6 to 7 minutes. Flip the tri-tip and sear the other side for another 6 to 7 minutes. Reduce the heat to medium-high or move the meat to indirect heat. Turn the meat again and grill for 8 to 10 minutes. Flip and grill again for an additional 5 to 6 minutes, until an instant-read thermometer reads 120°F (50°C) for rare, 130°F (55°C) for medium-rare, and 140°F (60°C) for medium. A 2-pound (910-g) tri-tip will need about 25 minutes total cooking time.

Remove from the grill and let rest on a cutting board for 15 to 20 minutes for the juices to redistribute.

While the meat is resting, warm each tortilla over an open flame until just starting to char. Alternatively, warm the tortillas in a microwave on 30-second bursts until warmed through. Slice the meat against the grain and serve with chipotle salsa, guacamole, and charred tortillas.

Serves 4 to 6 | Total Time: About 1 hour and 30 minutes (Prep: 5. Cook: 20 to 25.)

Cedar Plank Salmon with Blistered Tomatoes

I love a cedar plank—cooking your fish or shrimp on one gives it great, tender texture and infuses a subtle woodsy flavor without totally overpowering it. Normally you soak the plank in water before cooking with it, but recently my friend Adam suggested soaking it in white wine. (He's a genius!) Turns out that this little trick is the perfect way to give your fish another subtle layer of flavor (not to mention to get rid of that half-full bottle that's been sitting in your fridge a little too long).

Since I love serving this dish for company—it's the consummate impressive dish that really takes about twenty minutes—I wanted something easy but elegant to go alongside. These blistered tomatoes get a quick sauté with shallots and herbs, which keeps their texture intact and makes for a colorful accompaniment to the salmon.

Ingredients

For the salmon:

2 to 3 cups (480 to 720 ml) white wine
1 (2-pound/910-kg) salmon fillet, skin removed
2 tablespoons olive oil
2 tablespoons brown sugar
Kosher salt and freshly cracked black pepper
Lemon wedges
Torn fresh basil and flat-leaf parsley

For the blistered tomatoes:

1 tablespoon olive oil
2 shallots, thinly sliced
3 cloves garlic, sliced
1 quart (580 g) heirloom cherry tomatoes
Kosher salt and freshly cracked black pepper
½ cup (20 g) torn fresh basil leaves
¼ cup (13 g) fresh flat-leaf parsley leaves

Put a large cedar plank in a wide container or baking dish and add enough wine to cover it. Soak for 2 to 4 hours.

To make the blistered tomatoes: Using your heaviest large cast-iron skillet, heat the oil over high heat. Add the shallots and garlic and cook for 1 minute, or until fragrant. Add the cherry tomatoes and cook without moving them for 2 minutes, or until they start to blister. Give them a quick stir and let them sit for another 2 minutes or so. Season with salt and pepper and sprinkle with the basil and parsley. Set aside.

To make the salmon: Preheat an outdoor grill or grill pan to medium heat

Remove the cedar plank from the wine. Lay the salmon on top of the cedar plank, making sure it doesn't hang off the edges. Drizzle the salmon with the oil, sprinkle with the brown sugar, and season with salt and pepper. Place the cedar plank on the grill, cover, and grill for 12 to 15 minutes, until the salmon is uniformly pink in the center.

Using tongs or a large grill-safe spatula, transfer the salmon to a flat surface to rest. Top with the blistered tomatoes, a few squeezed lemon wedges, and some basil and parsley, and serve immediately.

Serves 6 | Total Time: At least 2 hours and 25 minutes
(Prep: 5. Cook: 20.)

Pesto Lasagna Bolognese

If there ever was a crowd-pleasing dish, it's a steaming hot, cheese-still-bubbling baking dish of lasagna. To give it a little more polish, I layer up no-cook lasagna sheets (which have great texture and save you a pot to clean) with bolognese, a decadent meat sauce with loads of flavor from pancetta, beef, pork, herbs, garlic, tomatoes, and red wine. Then I drizzle some basil vinaigrette over the top to balance out all that richness. It's also the ultimate make-ahead dish: you can assemble the lasagna the day before company comes and cook it off right before serving. Or store it in the freezer for a week and throw it in the oven when it's time to eat.

Ingredients

4 ounces (115 g) pancetta, finely chopped
1 medium onion, minced
1 medium stalk celery with leaves, minced
1 small carrot, minced
6 cloves garlic, roughly chopped
1 teaspoon dried oregano
1 teaspoon dried basil
1 pound (455 g) ground pork
1 pound (455 g) ground beef
⅔ cup (165 ml) dry red wine
1 cup (240 ml) milk
1 (28-ounce/840-g) can crushed tomatoes
1 cup (240 ml) tomato sauce
Kosher salt and freshly cracked black pepper
12 no-cook lasagna sheets (9 ounces)
1 pound (455 g) ricotta cheese
1 pound (455 g) whole-milk low-moisture shredded mozzarella cheese
½ cup (50 g) shredded Parmesan cheese
Basil Vinaigrette (page 250)

Heat a large Dutch oven over medium-high heat. Add the pancetta and cook, stirring frequently with a wooden spoon, for 5 minutes, or until some of the fat renders. Add the onion, celery, and carrot and cook for another 6 to 7 minutes, until the vegetables are softened and fragrant. Add the garlic, oregano, and basil and stir to combine. Add the ground meats and cook, stirring frequently, until deep brown in color. Add the wine, reduce the heat to medium-low, and cook, stirring occasionally, until the wine has reduced by half, about 5 minutes.

Stir in the milk, crushed tomatoes, and tomato sauce. Bring to a simmer over medium-high heat and then reduce to a simmer, cooking uncovered for about 1 hour, until the sauce resembles a thick, meaty stew. Season with salt and pepper.

Preheat the oven to 350°F (175°C).

Pour a thin layer of the meat sauce over a 9 by 13-inch (23 by 33-cm) baking dish. Top with 6 of the pasta sheets and another thin layer of meat sauce. Spoon on half of the ricotta for the next layer, followed by a layer of half of the mozzarella and half of the Parmesan. Slather the top with the basil vinaigrette. Add a final layer of pasta and the remaining meat sauce. Finish with the remaining ricotta, mozzarella, and Parmesan cheeses. Bake for 45 to 50 minutes, until the cheese is golden brown and bubbly. Remove from the oven and let rest for 10 minutes before serving.

Serves 10+ | Total Time: 2 hours and 30 minutes
(Prep: 15. Cook: 2 hours and 15 minutes.)

Chapter 8:

Carbs, Carbs + More Carbs

I am not exaggerating when I tell you that growing up, I ONLY ate grilled cheese and buttered noodles. Seriously, until I was fifteen that was pretty much all that was on the menu. Eventually I worked in other food groups, but I still love carbs in all shapes and sizes—pasta, bread, burgers, pizza . . . yeah, I'm gonna go make myself something to eat, and in the meantime, I'll leave you with these exceptionally crave-worthy recipes.

Bean, Cheese, *and* Chicken Tortas

I have two husbands: one is my actual husband, Thomas, and the other is my work husband, Matt. Thomas requests schnitzel on a daily basis . . . I kid you not. Matt, on the other hand, is Mexican American and grew up eating beans every night, so that's usually his request when I'm cooking. I came up with this recipe to keep both of them happy, plus a healthy helping of cheese for me.

Ingredients

- 4 (4- to 6-ounce/115- to 170-g) boneless, skinless chicken breasts
- 1 cup (125 g) all-purpose flour
- Kosher salt and freshly cracked black pepper
- Zest of 1 lemon
- 1 teaspoon garlic powder
- 2 large eggs, beaten
- 2 cups (160 g) panko bread crumbs
- ¼ cup (60 ml) olive oil
- 4 bolillo, telera, or hoagie rolls
- 4 tablespoons (60 ml) mayonnaise
- 1 cup (185 g) refried beans, warmed
- 8 ounces Oaxaca cheese, sliced
- 2 heirloom tomatoes, sliced
- 1 cup (55 g) shredded lettuce
- ½ red onion, thinly sliced
- 1 ripe avocado, pitted, peeled, and lightly mashed
- ¼ cup (25 g) pickled jalapeño chile slices
- Hot sauce

Place one chicken breast in a heavy-duty plastic bag and pound with a meat mallet (or the smooth part of a rolling pin) until it is about ½ inch (12 mm) thick, getting it as even as possible. Remove the pounded chicken breast from the bag and repeat with the remaining chicken breasts.

Prepare three bowls: one with flour, salt and pepper to taste, the lemon zest, and garlic powder, one with the beaten eggs, and the third with the panko.

Dredge one chicken breast in the flour, coating both sides and shaking off any excess. Next, dunk it into the beaten egg and let any excess drain off. Then coat it with the panko. Repeat with the remaining chicken breasts.

Place a large skillet over medium-high heat and add the oil. Once the oil is hot and shimmering, carefully place one chicken breast into the pan and cook for 3 to 4 minutes, until golden brown on the bottom. Flip it over and cook for an additional 3 to 4 minutes, until golden brown on the second side and cooked through. Remove the chicken to a paper towel–lined plate and repeat with the remaining chicken breasts.

To build the torta: Split the rolls and spread each with 1 tablespoon of the mayonnaise, then spread ¼ cup (45 g) refried beans over the bottom bun. Add a fried chicken cutlet, the cheese, tomato slices, lettuce, onion slices, mashed avocado, and pickled jalapeño. Serve with plenty of hot sauce!

Serves: 4 | Total Time: About 45 minutes (Prep: 15. Cook: 30.)

Triple Crème Grilled Cheese

One day Matt (my BFF and photographer) walked into the studio and professed that he had discovered the best grilled cheese in the entire world. Quite a bold statement in my presence considering that I ate grilled cheese every day growing up and my dad makes THE BEST grilled cheese on the planet—cut on a diagonal, of course. But I agreed to try Matt's sandwich, in the name of science. Admittedly, it was pretty good; just a more sophisticated version than Colby Jack cheese, wheat bread, and butter (with a side of ketchup). I used it as inspiration for this adult grilled cheese, which layers triple-crème brie, prosciutto, Marcona almonds, and honey on a French baguette.

Ingredients

Olive oil
1 French baguette, sliced in half lengthwise and cut into 4 equal pieces
2 to 3 tablespoons honey, wildflower if possible
12 ounces (340 g) triple-crème brie, at room temperature
8 slices prosciutto
½ cup (70 g) Marcona almonds

Heat a panini press or grill pan to high heat.

Lightly oil the tops and bottoms of the baguette. Drizzle the insides of the baguette with the honey and layer on slices of brie and prosciutto. Top with the almonds. Close the sandwiches, place in the panini press (if using a grill pan, place a clean skillet on top of the sandwiches to lightly press them), and cook for 3 to 5 minutes. If you're using a grill pan, flip the grilled cheese after 3 minutes and let the other side toast, until the sandwich is melty. Serve immediately.

Serves 4 | Total Time: 7 minutes (Prep: 2. Cook: 5.)

Pizza
for All Seasons

This is my favorite way to cook: go to the market, buy a bunch of stuff, and figure out how I can make it into a pizza. In the spring, it's all about light, fresh flavor combinations like asparagus and peas plus mozzarella, prosciutto, a couple perfectly sunny-side-up eggs, and a sprinkling of basil vinaigrette. Elote-inspired roasted corn, cotija cheese, and cilantro get top billing in the summer; pulled pork and cabbage slaw are put to use in the fall (inspired by giving second life to barbecue leftovers); and Brussels sprouts, bacon, and Havarti shine in the winter.

Pea Pizza (Spring)

All-purpose flour
½ cup (75 g) fresh peas
1 bunch asparagus, tips only
1 pound (455 g) fresh pizza dough
⅓ cup (75 ml) Basil Vinaigrette (page 250)
1 cup (110 g) fresh mozzarella cheese, sliced
2 large eggs
4 ounces (115 g) prosciutto
¼ cup (10 g) fresh basil leaves
Kosher salt and freshly cracked black pepper

Preheat the oven to 475°F (245°C). Lightly flour a rimless baking sheet or pizza peel.

While the oven is heating up, bring a small pot of water to a boil and prepare an ice bath. Add the peas to the boiling water and cook for 90 seconds. Remove and immediately dunk into the ice bath to cool. Set aside. Repeat the process for the asparagus tips, cooking for 2 to 3 minutes before dunking into the ice bath. Once both vegetables are cooled, remove and transfer to a paper towel–lined plate to dry.

On a clean, floured surface, shape the dough into 2 medium-ish rounds. Let the dough sit for 5 minutes, then re-form it to make sure it's as big as you'd like it to be. Place the dough on the prepared baking sheet or pizza peel.

Spread the basil vinaigrette over the top of each pizza. Top with the mozzarella and scatter the peas and asparagus on top of the cheese.

Transfer to the oven and bake for 5 to 6 minutes, until the crust just starts to puff. Remove the pizzas, carefully crack an egg onto the top of each pizza, and return to the oven for an additional 5 to 6 minutes, until the whites are set and the yolks are still soft. Remove from the oven, add the prosciutto, garnish with basil, season with salt and pepper, and serve immediately.

Serves 4 to 6 | Total Time: 20 to 22 minutes
(Prep: 10. Cook: 10 to 12.)

Street Corn Pizza (Summer)

All-purpose flour
1 pound (455 g) fresh pizza dough
¼ cup (60 ml) olive oil
4 cloves garlic, finely chopped
2 cups (220 g) shredded mozzarella cheese
1 cup (120 g) grated cotija cheese (or Parmesan)
1 cup (145 g) roasted or sautéed corn
Kosher salt and freshly cracked black pepper
1 teaspoon chili powder
3 to 4 tablespoons (8 to 10 g) fresh cilantro
Lime wedges
½ teaspoon red pepper flakes

Preheat the oven to 475°F (245°C). Lightly flour a rimless baking sheet or pizza peel.

On a clean, floured surface, shape the dough into 2 medium-ish rounds. Let the dough sit for 5 minutes, then re-form it to make sure it's as big as you'd like it to be. Place the dough on the prepared baking sheet or pizza peel.

Spread the oil over the top of each pizza and sprinkle with the garlic. Top the pizzas with the mozzarella, almost all of the cotija (reserve a little for garnish), and the corn. Season with salt and pepper.

Transfer the pizzas to the oven and bake for 10 to 12 minutes, until the cheese is fully melted and the crust is golden brown. Remove from the oven, season with salt and pepper, and top with the chili powder and cilantro. Sprinkle with the red pepper flakes and the remaining cotija cheese and serve with lime wedges to squeeze on top.

Serves 4 to 6 | Total Time: 20 to 22 minutes
(Prep: 10. Cook: 10 to 12.)

Pulled Pork Pizza with Cabbage Slaw *(Fall)*

All-purpose flour
1 pound (455 g) fresh pizza dough
⅓ cup (75 ml) Homemade BBQ Sauce (page 253)
1½ cups (160 g) shredded smoked Gouda cheese
1 cup (195 g) Pulled Pork (page 203)
1 cup (55 g) Cabbage Slaw (page 144)
Fresh cilantro
Sliced pickled jalapeño chiles
Kosher salt and freshly cracked black pepper

Preheat the oven to 475°F (245°C). Lightly flour a rimless baking sheet or pizza peel.

On a clean, floured surface, shape the dough into 2 medium-ish rounds. Let the dough sit for 5 minutes, then re-form it to make sure it's as big as you'd like it to be. Place the dough on the prepared baking sheet or pizza peel.

Spread the BBQ sauce over the top of each pizza. Top with the shredded cheese and scatter the pulled pork on top of the cheese.

Transfer to the oven and bake for 10 to 12 minutes, until the cheese is fully melted and the crust is golden brown. Remove the pizza from the oven and top with the slaw, cilantro, and pickled jalapeños. Season with salt and pepper, and serve immediately.

Serves 4 to 6 | Total Time: 15 to 17 minutes
(Prep: 5. Cook: 10 to 12.)

Shaved Brussels Sprouts and Bacon Pizza (Winter)

All-purpose flour
1 pound (455 g) pizza dough
¼ cup (60 ml) olive oil
6 to 8 cloves garlic, finely chopped
Kosher salt and freshly cracked black pepper
2 cups (220 g) shredded Havarti cheese
1 cup (90 g) shaved Brussels sprouts, plus more for garnish
4 strips applewood-smoked bacon, cooked and crumbled
Red pepper flakes
2 to 3 tablespoons chopped fresh chives

Preheat the oven to 475°F (245°C). Lightly flour a rimless baking sheet or pizza peel.

On a clean, floured surface, shape the dough into 2 medium-ish rounds. Let the dough sit for 5 minutes, then re-form it to make sure it's as big as you'd like it to be. Place the dough on the prepared baking sheet or pizza peel.

Spread the oil over the top of each pizza and sprinkle with the garlic. Season with salt and pepper. Top the pizzas with the shredded cheese and scatter the shredded Brussels sprouts and bacon on top of the cheese.

Transfer to the oven and bake for 10 to 12 minutes, until the cheese is fully melted and the crust is golden brown. Remove from the oven and adjust the salt and pepper as needed. Sprinkle with the red pepper flakes, some shredded Brussels sprouts, and the chives and serve.

Serves 4 to 6 | Total Time: 20 to 22 minutes
(Prep: 10. Cook: 10 to 12.)

Pepperoni and Jalapeño Pizza (All Seasons)

This recipe is the brainchild of Adam, food stylist to the stars. He figured out that if you put the sauce on top of the cheese, it keeps the crust from getting soggy while the caramelized cheese-topped crust bits are like the best cheesy bread sticks you'd normally order late-night. It's my new go-to pizza recipe for any time of the year.

All-purpose flour
1 pound (455 g) pizza dough
10 deli slices mozzarella cheese
1 cup (240 ml) pizza sauce
15 to 20 slices pepperoni
1 teaspoon crushed red pepper flakes, or to taste
1 jalapeño chile, thinly sliced
Kosher salt and freshly cracked black pepper

Preheat the oven to 475°F (245°C). Lightly flour a rimless baking sheet or pizza peel.

On a clean, floured surface, shape the dough into 2 medium-ish rounds. Let the dough sit for 5 minutes, then re-form it to make sure it's as big as you'd like it to be. Place the dough on the prepared baking sheet or pizza peel.

Distribute the mozzarella on top of the crusts. Spread the pizza sauce over the cheese and scatter with the pepperoni, red pepper flakes, and sliced jalapeños.

Transfer the pizzas to the oven and bake for 10 to 12 minutes, until the cheese has melted and the crust is golden brown. Remove from the oven and season with salt, pepper, and extra red pepper flakes if you like. Serve immediately.

Serves 4 | Total Time: 15 minutes (Prep: 5. Cook: 10 to 12.)

Cheesy Pulled Pork Sandwiches with Jalapeño Slaw

If I'm having a huge crew over for some backyard fun, this is definitely on the menu. It's an amped-up take on classic barbecue flavors, with creamy Havarti cheese and spicy jalapeño slaw. It also feeds a lot of people, so you can either serve these up as big-ass sandwiches for a smaller group or make them slider-size for a crowd.

Ingredients

For the pulled pork:

2½ pounds (1 kg) pork shoulder
Homemade BBQ Sauce (page 253)

For the jalapeño slaw:

½ head red cabbage, shredded
½ head green cabbage, shredded
4 scallions, white and light green parts, thinly sliced
1 jalapeño chile, finely diced
1 tablespoon Dijon mustard
1 clove garlic, minced
⅓ cup (75 ml) olive oil
¼ cup (60 ml) apple cider vinegar
2 tablespoons fresh lime juice
1 tablespoon honey
Kosher salt and freshly cracked black pepper

For serving:

6 to 8 brioche burger buns, buttered and toasted
1 avocado, pitted, peeled, and mashed
12 to 16 slices Havarti cheese

To make the pulled pork: Combine the pork and BBQ sauce in a slow cooker and mix to coat the pork in the sauce. Cook for 8 hours on low, or until fork-tender. Uncover and, using two forks, shred the pork and transfer the pork with the remaining sauce into a large bowl.

To make the slaw: In a large bowl, combine the cabbages, scallions, and jalapeño. In a small bowl, whisk the mustard, garlic, oil, vinegar, lime juice, and honey together to dissolve the honey. Season with salt and pepper. Toss with the cabbage mixture and let sit for 30 minutes.

Preheat the broiler.

To assemble: Place the bottom buns on a large baking sheet and slather with the smashed avocado. Top with the pulled pork and finish with 2 slices of Havarti cheese each. Place under the broiler and broil until the cheese is melted, about 1 minute. Top with some of the slaw and the top bun. Use a toothpick to secure if needed and serve immediately.

Serves 6 to 8 | Total Time: 8 hours and 11 minutes
(Prep: 10. Cook: 8 hours and 1 minute.)

Sun-Dried Tomato Turkey Burgers with Balsamic Onions

Turkey burgers are one of the trickiest recipes I've tried to perfect. Turkey easily gets dried out and doesn't exactly pack a ton of flavor. But it's an awesome protein option if you want to keep things on the lighter side, and because it is so mild, it's a great canvas for bigger, bolder ingredients. I figured out that stuffing the patties with Parmesan cheese and sun-dried tomatoes really helps in the flavor department, while topping the burgers with melty mozzarella and sweet-salty balsamic onions keeps the whole affair nice and juicy.

Ingredients

For the balsamic onions:

2 yellow onions, cut into ¼-inch (6-mm) slices
¼ cup (60 ml) balsamic vinegar
2 tablespoons olive oil

For the turkey burgers:

1 pound (455 g) 85% fat ground dark meat turkey
2 cloves garlic, finely chopped
1 shallot, finely diced
¼ cup (11 g) chopped fresh chives
¼ cup (25 g) shredded Parmesan cheese
¼ cup (30 g) finely diced sun-dried tomatoes packed in olive oil
1 teaspoon red pepper flakes
1 teaspoon kosher salt
½ teaspoon freshly cracked black pepper

For assembly:

4 slices deli mozzarella
4 brioche buns, split and toasted
1 beefsteak tomato, cut into 4 slices
1 cup (20 g) arugula
2 to 4 tablespoons (30 to 60 ml) balsamic glaze

To make the balsamic onions: Preheat the oven to 400°F (205°C).

Toss the onions, vinegar, and oil on a large baking sheet and transfer to the oven. Roast for 25 to 30 minutes, until softened.

To make the turkey burgers: Preheat an outdoor grill or grill pan to medium heat.

Put the ground turkey in a large bowl and add the garlic, shallot, chives, Parmesan, sun-dried tomatoes, red pepper flakes, salt, and pepper. Using your hands, incorporate all the ingredients into the ground turkey, taking care not to overmix. Form the mixture into four ½-inch (12-mm) thick patties.

To cook and assemble: Grill the burgers until cooked through, 5 to 7 minutes per side, melting on the mozzarella during the last minute. Place the burgers on the toasted buns, add the sliced tomato, balsamic onions, arugula, and balsamic glaze, and finish with the top bun. Serve immediately.

Serves 4 | Total Time: 55 minutes (Prep: 10. Cook: 45.)

Adam's Meatball Subs

Remember those epic meatballs that I was raving about (page 173)? Well, the only thing that makes them better is reheating leftovers with tons of mozzarella cheese and stuffing the whole mess into Italian-style rolls. Sunday supper is served! Adam made these for me a few years back and life has been better ever since!

Ingredients

6 Italian-style rolls
Olive oil
1 clove garlic, peeled
Perfect Meatballs with Cherry Tomato Sauce (page 173)
Basil Vinaigrette (page 250)
1 pound (455 g) fresh or low-moisture mozzarella cheese, sliced about ¼ inch (6 mm) thick
½ cup (65 g) caramelized onions (see Bruschetta Bar, page 23)
½ cup (30 g) Garlic Wild Mushrooms (page 116)
Parmesan cheese

Preheat the oven to 350°F (175°C).

Warm the rolls in the oven for 10 minutes. Slice off and discard the ends of each roll. Cut the rolls in half lengthwise.

Drizzle the cut sides of the top and bottom roll halves with oil and rub with the garlic until fragrant. Arrange the bottom roll halves on a baking sheet, cut side up. Spoon a generous layer of the tomato sauce mixture from the meatballs onto each of the bottom halves and add a drizzle of basil vinaigrette. Slice the meatballs in half if needed and arrange on the sandwiches, overlapping as necessary for even coverage.

Lay the mozzarella slices on top of the meatballs. Transfer the baking sheet to the oven and bake until the mozzarella is fully melted, about 5 minutes, warming the top halves of the rolls in the oven for the last minute. Add a few tablespoons of caramelized onions and mushrooms and grate Parmesan all over. Drizzle with basil vinaigrette and serve immediately.

Serves 6 | Total Time: 20 minutes (Prep: 5. Cook: 15.)

Spaghetti *with* Castelvetrano Olive Tapenade

Olives are a whole food group in my book, and as I've mentioned before, castelvetranos are my absolute favorites. So it only makes sense to combine them with my other true love: pasta. Pasta is pretty much all I ate until I was fifteen years old, but this recipe is definitely an adult upgrade. It calls for tossing spaghetti noodles with salty, briny olive tapenade plus toasted bread crumbs for texture and a small heap of Parmesan cheese to tie everything together. Also—side note—I normally HATE tapenade because they always seem to be made with black olives and those aren't my jam, but trust me on this one, it's EVERYTHING!

Ingredients

1 cup (155 g) castelvetrano olives, plus extra crushed olives for topping
2 teaspoons drained capers
2 cloves garlic, peeled
¼ cup (13 g) chopped fresh flat-leaf parsley
¼ cup (10 g) chopped fresh basil
Zest and juice of 1 lemon
½ teaspoon red pepper flakes
1 teaspoon kosher salt
½ teaspoon freshly cracked black pepper
10 ounces spaghetti or angel hair pasta
2 tablespoons olive oil
½ cup (50 g) grated Parmesan cheese
½ cup (50 g) toasted sourdough bread crumbs

Remove the pits from the olives the same way you would crush a clove of garlic: Using the flat, wide side of your knife, press down on the olive until it breaks open. Remove the pit and discard it. Repeat for the remaining olives, then place the olives in a high-powered blender. Add the capers, garlic, parsley, basil, lemon zest, red pepper flakes, salt, and pepper. Pulse for about 1 minute, until chunky.

Cook the pasta according to the package directions for al dente. Drain and set aside.

In a large skillet, heat the oil over medium heat. Add the olive tapenade mixture and cook for 1 minute, or until fragrant. Add the cooked pasta, the lemon juice, and Parmesan and toss to combine. Adjust the salt and pepper as needed, top with the bread crumbs and crushed olives, and serve.

Serves 4 | Total Time: 20 minutes (Prep: 10. Cook: 10.)

Cheese-Belly Chicken Burgers with Sour Cream and Guacamole

It's easy to get stuck in the tomato-onion-pickle-ketchup rut (total classic, total snooze), so why not shake up your grill-out game? This juicy chicken burger is not only stuffed with cheddar cheese, garlic, spices, and jalapeño; it's decked out with sour cream, guac, and salsa. Chicken. Burger. Game changer (though feel free to use beef instead of chicken).

Ingredients

1½ pounds (680 g) ground chicken
½ cup (65 g) finely chopped yellow onion
¼ cup (10 g) finely chopped fresh cilantro
2 cloves garlic, finely chopped
2 teaspoons chopped jalapeño chile
1 teaspoon ground cumin
1 teaspoon paprika
⅓ cup (40 g) finely shredded cheddar cheese
Kosher salt and freshly cracked black pepper
4 burger buns, split and toasted
½ cup (120 ml) sour cream
4 leaves butter lettuce
¼ red onion, thinly sliced
½ cup (85 g) chipotle salsa
1 cup (155 g) Gaby's Famous Guacamole (page 27)

Preheat an outdoor grill or grill pan to medium heat.

Put the ground chicken in a medium bowl. Add the onion, cilantro, garlic, jalapeño, cumin, paprika, and cheese and season with salt and pepper. Use your hands to incorporate the ingredients into the chicken, making sure not to overmix.

Form the mixture into four ½-inch (12-mm) thick patties. Grill the burgers until cooked through, 5 to 7 minutes per side.

Serve each patty in a burger bun topped with sour cream, lettuce, sliced red onion, chipoltle salsa, and guacamole.

Serves 4 | Total Time: 24 minutes (Prep: 10. Cook: 14.)

Chicken Parmesan Pappardelle

The first thing I ever learned to cook was chicken Parm. I would make it at least three times a week and serve it to everyone—my college roommates, my tennis teammates, my then-boyfriend, and so on. It's such a comforting dish, and one I'm really fond of, so I wanted to figure out how to make it a little more polished for serving at a party. I took all the signature parts—marinara sauce, mozzarella cheese, Italian seasoning—and tossed it with pappardelle along with ground chicken!

Ingredients

1 tablespoon olive oil
3 to 4 cloves garlic, finely chopped
½ teaspoon red pepper flakes
1¼ pounds (565 g) ground chicken (white or dark meat, or ground turkey)
2 teaspoons dried Italian seasoning
Kosher salt and freshly cracked black pepper
1 (26-ounce/780-ml) jar marinara sauce
1 cup (100 g) shredded Parmesan cheese, plus more to garnish
1 cup (110 g) shredded mozzarella cheese
12 ounces (340 g) pappardelle pasta
Small fresh basil leaves

Heat the oil in a large skillet over medium-high heat. Add the garlic and red pepper flakes and cook for 2 to 3 minutes, until the garlic is fragrant. Add the ground chicken and Italian seasoning and season with salt and pepper. Cook, breaking up the chicken with the back of a wooden spoon, until it is in small pieces. Continue to cook until the chicken is cooked through, about 10 more minutes.

Add the marinara sauce, bring to a simmer, then reduce the heat to medium-low and simmer for 20 minutes. Reduce the heat to low, add the Parmesan and mozzarella cheeses, and stir to combine. Taste and adjust the salt and pepper as needed.

While the sauce is simmering, cook the pasta according to the package directions for al dente. Drain the pasta and transfer to the skillet with the meat sauce. Stir to coat the pasta in the sauce and serve garnished with basil leaves and additional Parmesan.

Serves 4 | Total Time: 45 minutes (Prep: 10. Cook: 35.)

Chapter 9:

Sweet Treats

The Dalkin clan has a major sweet tooth. My grandma always had brownies on offer when I visited, and my dad is pretty much the king of cookies. This love of all things baked definitely didn't skip a generation—I've yet to meet a cookie, brownie, or bar that I didn't like. But while I love to indulge in fancy-pants desserts from time to time, I say we leave those to the pastry chefs. For me, it's all about keeping things simple but decadent.

Giant Pavlova *with* Lemon Curd, Chantilly Cream, *and Fresh* Berries

This light-as-a-cloud dessert might have been made famous by the Australians (or Kiwis depending on who you ask, but I'm staying out of that debate), but I'm giving it a California-Girl makeover by adding a dose of sunny citrus and fresh berries. It's a particularly great dessert for summer (though feel free to change up the fruit topping depending on the season), and it's perfect for feeding a crowd—especially because you can make it in advance.

Just a couple rules of thumb: For fluffiest results, avoid making pavlova on high-humidity or rainy days and always wipe down the mixer bowl with white vinegar, which will ensure that no fat from previous baking was left behind (a definite egg-white downer). And get creative! Any combination of puddings, jams, curds, fruit, and whipped cream will work with this wonderfully sweet, crunchy-yet-soft pavlova shell.

Ingredients

For the meringue:

1¼ cups (245 g) superfine sugar
½ cup (65 g) powdered sugar
6 large egg whites
Pinch of kosher salt
Pinch of cream of tartar
1 teaspoon white vinegar
1 teaspoon vanilla extract

For the strawberries:

1 pint (290 g) strawberries, cleaned and hulled
2 tablespoons granulated sugar

For the Chantilly cream and lemon curd:

1½ cups (360 ml) heavy cream, chilled
½ cup (65 g) powdered sugar
½ teaspoon vanilla extract
½ cup (120 ml) lemon curd

To make the meringue: Preheat the oven to 230°F. Line a baking sheet with parchment paper, use a pencil to draw a 9-inch (23-cm) circle on the paper, then flip it over.

In a small bowl, combine the superfine sugar with the powdered sugar. Set aside.

In the very clean bowl of a stand mixer, combine the egg whites, salt, and cream of tartar. Start mixing on low speed, then gradually increase the speed to high once you see a nice froth starting, about 2 minutes. Continue beating on high speed until you have nice firm peaks. Then add the superfine sugar and powdered sugar mixture by the heaping tablespoon and continue beating until stiff and shiny, 6 to 8 minutes. Turn off the mixer and remove the bowl from the stand. Rub the mixture between your fingers; if it feels gritty, continue mixing until smooth.

Gently fold in the vinegar and vanilla, taking care not to let the egg whites deflate. Scoop the meringue onto the parchment-lined baking sheet into a mound to fill the circle outline. Create a slight indention in the top. Smear a little meringue in the 4 corners of the parchment (this will keep it from sliding).

(ingredients and recipe continue)

For the toppings:
1 cup (125 g) fresh raspberries
1 cup (145 g) fresh blueberries
Mint or edible flowers

Place in the oven and bake for 1 hour and 45 minutes. Turn off the oven and let the meringue rest in the oven for at least 2 hours or overnight. DON'T OPEN THE OVEN. The sudden drop in temperature might cause the pavlova to crack.

To make the strawberries: Slice half of the strawberries, put them in a medium bowl, and toss them with the granulated sugar. Pop in the fridge while the pavlova bakes. You want them to rest for about 2 hours, or overnight if time allows, to get super-saucy.

To make the Chantilly cream and lemon curd: In a chilled bowl of a stand mixer, combine the cream, powdered sugar, and vanilla. Start mixing on low speed and gradually increase the speed to medium high; continue mixing until the cream forms soft peaks. Turn off the mixer and set aside.

In a small bowl, mix the lemon curd and ½ cup (120 ml) of the whipped cream. Stir until combined and the lemon curd has a lightened texture.

To build the pavlova: Carefully move the cooled meringue from the baking sheet to a serving platter. Spoon on the lightened lemon curd and top with whipped cream. Spoon on the macerated strawberries, reserving some of the juice for topping. Top with the remaining (unmacerated) strawberries, the raspberries, and blueberries. Drizzle with reserved strawberry juices and serve. Garnish with mint or edible flowers.

Serves 10+ | Total Time: About 4 hours
(Prep: 15. Cook: 1 hour and 45 minutes.)

Strawberry Shortcakes

There's a berry stand at the LA farmers' market from a family farm called Harry's Berries, where the berries are so incredible that there have been legit brawls over who can scoop some up before they're sold out. I totally get it; the berries—which they've been growing since 1967—are so sweet and perfect that they rival any candy. So when you put them on a shortcake, this stand-by dessert becomes a whole new ball game. To do the berries justice, I pair them with a lemon-infused shortcake and plop a big dollop of freshly whipped cream on top.

Ingredients

For the strawberries:

1 pound (455 g) fresh strawberries, hulled and sliced
⅓ cup (65 g) granulated sugar

For the biscuits:

3 cups (375 g) all-purpose flour
2 teaspoons lemon zest
3 tablespoons granulated sugar
1½ tablespoons baking powder
1 teaspoon kosher salt
¾ cup (1½ sticks/170 g) cold unsalted butter, cut into small pieces
1½ cups (360 g) heavy cream
1½ teaspoons vanilla extract

For the cream:

2 cups (480 ml) heavy cream
⅔ cup (85 g) powdered sugar
Seeds of 1 vanilla bean

To make the strawberries: Combine the strawberries and sugar in a large bowl and toss to coat. Refrigerate for at least 2 hours, or overnight if time allows, until juicy.

To make the biscuits: In a food processor, combine the flour, lemon zest, sugar, baking powder, and salt. Pulse for 30 seconds, or until the ingredients are evenly combined. Add the butter and pulse for 20 to 30 seconds, until the butter is cut into pea-size chunks. Add the cream and vanilla to the food processor and process for 30 seconds, or until you have a dough. Remove the dough from the food processor and divide it into 9 equal portions about 3 ounces each. Form each portion of dough into a biscuit about ¾ inch (2 cm) thick. Transfer the biscuits to a baking sheet lined with parchment paper and chill for 20 minutes in the fridge.

While the biscuits chill, preheat the oven to 400°F (205°C).

Place the baking sheet in the oven and bake until the biscuits are medium golden brown, about 25 minutes. Remove from the oven and transfer to a cooling rack to cool.

To make the cream: Combine the cream, powdered sugar, and vanilla bean seeds in a large stand mixer and whip until medium stiff peaks form.

To assemble: Slice the biscuits in half. Top the bottom of each biscuit with a large spoonful of the strawberries. Place the top half of the biscuit on top of each and finish with a large dollop of the cream. Serve immediately.

Serves 9 | Total Time: 2 hours and 55 minutes
(Prep: 15. Cook: 25.)

Chocolate Chip S'mookies

Growing up, there were always cookies around. My dad, the aforementioned cookie monster, regularly made batches and stored them in the freezer so a sweet fix was never more than thirty seconds away. I've brought that same tradition into my own home, much to Thomas's delight. This recipe, which is a regular in the rotation, is inspired by summer nights spent around a campfire toasting marshmallows. Instead of graham crackers, a marshmallow filling gets sandwiched between two chocolate chip cookies. You will need a disposable piping bag and a ½-inch (12-mm) round or star piping tip for this recipe.

Ingredients

For the cookies:

1 cup (2 sticks/450 g) unsalted butter, at room temperature
1 cup (220 g) brown sugar
1 cup (200 g) granulated sugar
2 large eggs
2 teaspoons vanilla extract
2½ cups (315 g) all-purpose flour
1 teaspoon kosher salt
1 teaspoon baking soda
1 teaspoon baking powder
1 cup (175 g) chocolate chips
3 graham crackers, chopped

For the marshmallow filling:

½ cup (120 ml) water
1½ tablespoons unflavored gelatin
¾ cup (150 g) granulated sugar
½ cup (120 ml) light corn syrup
Pinch of kosher salt
½ teaspoon vanilla extract
Nonstick cooking spray

To make the cookie dough: In a stand mixer, cream together the butter, brown sugar, and granulated sugar on low until smooth, 2 to 3 minutes. Add the eggs and vanilla, scraping down the sides of the mixing bowl, and mix until incorporated. Add the flour, salt, baking soda, and baking powder and mix on low speed until all the ingredients are incorporated. Stir in the chocolate chips and graham crackers by hand. Cover the dough with plastic wrap and refrigerate for at least 2 hours or up to 72 hours.

To make the marshmallow filling: While the dough is chilling, combine ¼ cup (60 ml) of the water and the gelatin in the bowl of a stand mixer. Fit the mixer with the whisk attachment.

In a small saucepan, combine the remaining ¼ cup (60 ml) water, the granulated sugar, corn syrup, and salt. Bring to a boil over medium-high heat, stirring until the sugar has dissolved and brushing down the sides of the pan with a pastry brush dipped in water to wash any sugar crystals down into the syrup. Attach a candy thermometer to the saucepan and continue to cook without stirring until the sugar mixture reads 240°F (115°C). Remove from the heat, remove the thermometer, and with the mixer set to low speed, slowly pour the hot sugar mixture into the mixer. Once all of the sugar mixture is in, increase the speed to high and mix for 5 minutes. Add the vanilla and mix for 1 minute.

To bake the cookies: Preheat the oven to 350°F (175°C). Line 2 baking sheets with parchment paper.

(ingredients and recipe continue)

Scoop out 2 tablespoons of the dough and roll the dough into a ball. Place the dough onto the prepared baking sheets; 12 cookies per sheet. Bake for 10 to 12 minutes, until the edges are just slightly golden brown and the center is still a bit soft.

Remove the baking sheets from the oven and let the cookies rest for about 5 minutes before transferring them to a wire cooling rack. Cool the sheets and repeat with the remaining dough (makes 36 cookies total).

To assemble: Using a rubber spatula sprayed with cooking spray (to keep the marshmallow from sticking), remove the marshmallow filling from the mixer and place it in a piping bag fitted with a ½-inch (12-mm) round or star tip. Pipe some marshmallow onto the bottom of a cookie, then sandwich with another cookie. Repeat with the remaining cookies and marshmallow. Serve as needed, but enjoy within 2 to 3 days.

Serves 16+ | Total Time: At least 2 hours and 50 minutes (Prep: 30. Cook: 10 to 20.)

Chocolate-Covered Strawberry Cheesecake Ice Pops

This recipe takes traditional cheesecake components—sweet and creamy cake; graham cracker crust; and fruit compote topping—and reimagines them as an adorable dessert on a stick. They're perfect for summer parties or just passing around on a warm afternoon. You will need ice pop sticks and 2½-ounce (75-ml) molds or 3-ounce (90-ml) paper cups for this recipe.

Ingredients

8 ounces fresh strawberries, hulled and diced
¼ cup (50 g) granulated sugar
1 (8-ounce/225-g) package cream cheese, at room temperature
¼ cup (60 ml) full-fat sour cream
½ cup (65 g) powdered sugar
⅓ cup (75 ml) milk
½ teaspoon vanilla extract
¾ cup (130 g) dark chocolate chips
3 tablespoons coconut oil
1 graham cracker, pulverized in a food processor
¼ cup (40 g) freeze-dried strawberries, pulverized in a food processor

In a small saucepan, combine the strawberries and granulated sugar. Place over medium-high heat and cook until the mixture resembles a chunky jam, 8 to 10 minutes. Remove from heat and let cool completely.

In a food processor, combine the cream cheese, sour cream, powdered sugar, milk, and vanilla and process until silky. Transfer to a large bowl and lightly fold in half of the strawberry mixture.

Fill the ice pop molds halfway with the cheesecake mixture, layer in a spoonful of strawberry jam, and top off with the cheesecake mixture.

Place in the freezer for 30 minutes, then remove from the freezer and insert wooden sticks. Return to the freezer and freeze until solid, about 4 hours.

Make the chocolate topping by combining the chocolate chips and oil in a small glass bowl. Microwave for 1 minute, then stir. Continue melting at 10-second intervals until fully melted. Let sit for 15 minutes before assembling.

Line a baking sheet with parchment paper. Working quickly, remove a pop from its mold (a dip in hot water helps) and dip into the melted chocolate. Quickly sprinkle with graham crackers and freeze-dried strawberries and place on the prepared baking sheet. Place the pops back in the freezer and keep them there until serving.

Serves 8 | Total Time: 4 hours and 55 minutes
(Prep: 25. Chill: 4 hours and 30 minutes.)

Palm Springs Date Shake

One of my favorite parts of rolling in to Palm Springs during the summer—aside from the obligatory visits to In-N-Out Burger (page 161)—is pulling over at one of the many date shake stops. This rich, thick shake has been a staple of the Palm Springs scene since the late twenties, when there were more dates than the farmers knew what to do with. So they opened roadside shacks offering what were essentially milkshakes with dates blended in, which gave them extra sweetness. I like staying true to the original recipe (though I do add a touch of honey to round things out), but feel free to get creative with what kind of ice cream you use—if cookies 'n' cream ice cream makes its way into your shake, I wouldn't be mad!

Ingredients

4 Medjool dates, pitted and roughly chopped
1 cup (240 ml) milk (dairy, almond, cashew, hemp, or soy)
2 cups (300 g) vanilla ice cream (or coffee or chocolate ice cream)
1 teaspoon honey

In a blender, combine the dates and milk and blend until smooth and very frothy. Add the ice cream and honey and pulse a few times, until smooth. Pour into two glasses and serve immediately.

Serves 2 | Total Time: 2 minutes (Prep: 2. Cook: 0.)

Raspberry–White Chocolate Cheesecake Cookie Bars

When it comes to choosing which desserts I'm going to add to my arsenal of recipes, I almost always stick to the unfussy classics—cakes, cookies, bars, and, in this case, cheesecake cookie bars! This recipe blends the dense, pan-baked goodness of a bar with layers of cheesecake and cookie dough that are dotted with white chocolate and fresh raspberries. There is no bake-off or bake sale that you can't win with these.

Ingredients

For the cookie layer:

1 cup (2 sticks/225 g) unsalted butter, at room temperature
½ cup (110 g) brown sugar
1½ cups (300 g) granulated sugar
2 large eggs
2½ teaspoons vanilla extract
2½ cups (315 g) all-purpose flour
1 teaspoon kosher salt
1 teaspoon baking soda
1 teaspoon baking powder
1¼ cups (205 g) white chocolate chips
1 cup (125 g) fresh raspberries

For the cheesecake layer:

8 ounces (225 g) cream cheese, at room temperature
½ cup (100 g) granulated sugar
1 large egg
1 teaspoon vanilla extract

To make the cookie layer: In a stand mixer, cream together the butter, brown sugar, and granulated sugar for 3 minutes, until smooth. Add the eggs and vanilla and continue to mix, scraping down the sides of the bowl. Add the flour, salt, baking soda, and baking powder and mix on low speed until the ingredients are incorporated. Fold in 1 cup (165 g) of the white chocolate chips.

To make the cheesecake layer: In a food processor, combine the cream cheese, granulated sugar, egg, and vanilla and mix for 2 minutes, scraping down the sides as needed, until the ingredients are evenly combined and the mixture is very smooth.

Preheat the oven to 350°F (175°C). Line a 9 by 13-inch (23 by 33-cm) baking pan with parchment paper with a little hanging over the sides. Press slightly more than half of the cookie dough mixture into the bottom of the pan to make one even layer. Spread the cheesecake mixture on top of the cookie dough. Crumble the remaining cookie dough and sprinkle it on top of the cheesecake mixture, then sprinkle with the remaining ¼ cup (40 g) white chocolate chips and the raspberries.

Place in the oven and bake for 40 to 45 minutes, until the cookie dough is golden brown. Remove the bars from the oven and let cool for 30 minutes. Transfer them to the fridge for at least 2 hours, or overnight if time allows (don't skip this part). Cut into bars and serve.

Serves 12+ | Total Time: About 2 hours and 55 minutes
(Prep: 10. Cook: 40 to 45.)

Flourless Chocolate Ice Cream Layer Cake

Summer birthdays can be kind of a bummer when you're a kid because school's out and your friends are all on vacation. So as an adult I feel like I owe it to myself to do it up right for my special day. This cake tends to make an appearance because it's the ultimate party cake: a layer of vanilla ice cream between sheets of flourless chocolate cake, topped with a drizzle of caramel sauce and scoops of more ice cream. Happy birthday to me!

Ingredients

For the cake layers:

2 cups (4 sticks/450 g) unsalted butter, plus more for greasing pans
1 pound (455 g) semisweet chocolate chips
2½ cups (500 g) sugar
2 cups (190 g) unsweetened cocoa powder
12 large eggs

For the ice cream layer:

1 quart (600 g) vanilla ice cream, slightly softened

For the caramel sauce:

1½ cups (300 g) sugar
¼ cup (60 ml) water
1 cup (240 ml) heavy cream
2 tablespoons unsalted butter

For the topping:

Lots and lots of ice cream scoops

To make the cake: Preheat the oven to 350°F (175°C). Butter two 10-inch (25-cm) springform pans and line the bottoms with waxed paper.

Combine the butter and chocolate in a large, heavy saucepan. Place over low heat and stir until melted. Add the sugar and cocoa powder and whisk to combine. Whisk in the eggs. Divide the batter between the prepared pans. Bake until a cake tester inserted into the center comes out clean, about 45 minutes. Place the cakes on wire racks to cool completely. Run a knife around the sides of the pans to loosen the cakes, then release the springform.

To make the ice cream layer: Line the bottom of another 10-inch (25-cm) springform pan (or wash one of the earlier ones) with plastic wrap on the inside and outside. Spread the softened ice cream into the pan in an even layer. Transfer the pan to the freezer and freeze until very firm, at least 4 hours or, preferably, overnight.

To make the caramel sauce: In a medium saucepan, combine the sugar and water. Place over low heat and heat until the sugar dissolves. Increase the heat and bring to a boil; boil without stirring until the syrup is deep amber in color, about 7 minutes. Remove from the heat. Add the cream (step away, as the mixture will bubble vigorously). Return to low heat and stir until any bits of caramel dissolve. Add the butter and whisk until smooth.

To assemble: Remove the ice cream layer from the springform pan. Working quickly so the ice cream doesn't melt,

(recipe continues)

place a chocolate cake layer on a cake plate, add the ice cream layer, then top with the remaining cake layer. You might need to freeze the layers after adding the ice cream if it gets too warm. Once all three layers are assembled, drizzle the cake with the warm caramel sauce. Pile up with scoops of ice cream and serve immediately.

Serves 12+ | Total Time: About 5 hours and 15 minutes (Prep: 15. Cook: 1 hour.)

Mocha-Chocolate Chunk Brownies

Whenever I knew we'd be visiting my grandma in Chicago, I'd call her to place an order for a batch of her famous brownies. By the time we got to her house, there'd be a pan of them waiting on the counter, still warm and sugar-dusted to perfection. I wanted to come up with my own recipe so I could channel those vibes whenever I was in the mood, and I've added espresso powder and chocolate chunks to make them even more rich and decadent. Mint chip ice cream optional. Grandma Dalkin would totally approve.

Ingredients

Nonstick cooking spray
10 tablespoons (1¼ sticks/150 g) unsalted butter
1¼ (250 g) cups sugar
2 teaspoons instant espresso powder
¾ cup (70 g) unsweetened cocoa powder
½ teaspoon Maldon salt
2 teaspoons vanilla extract
2 large eggs
½ cup (65 g) all-purpose flour
1 cup (170 g) dark chocolate chunks
Mint chip ice cream for serving, if desired

Preheat the oven to 350°F (175°C). Spray a 9 by 9-inch (23 by 23-cm) baking pan with cooking spray and line it with parchment paper.

In a large saucepan, combine the butter, sugar, espresso powder, cocoa powder, and salt. Place over medium heat and cook, stirring, for 2 minutes, or until the butter is melted. Remove from the heat, as you do not want the eggs to curdle when added, and add the vanilla and eggs. Stir to combine. Stir in the flour and chocolate chunks. Pour the batter into the prepared pan and bake for 30 minutes. The brownies will still have a bit of wiggle when they are removed from the oven, but they will firm up once cooled.

Remove from the oven, place on a wire rack, and let cool to room temperature. Transfer to the refrigerator and chill for at least 1 hour or overnight, then slice and serve. Add a scoop of mint chip ice cream if desired.

Serves 9 to 16 | Total Time: At least 1 hour and 35 minutes (Prep: 5. Cook: 30.)

Summer Fruit Galette

As I mentioned earlier, in the case of Stone Fruit with Burrata (page 100), stone fruit season is a BIG deal in my world. I go through peaches, plums, nectarines, and apricots by the bucket load. You can use any kind of stone fruit for this galette and it's not only going to be delicious but beautiful, too. Enormous scoops of ice cream optional.

Ingredients

For the pie dough:

1⅓ (165 g) cups all-purpose flour
1 tablespoon granulated sugar
¼ teaspoon kosher salt
½ cup (1 stick/115 g) cold unsalted butter
3 to 4 tablespoons (45 to 60 ml) ice-cold water

For the filling:

1½ pounds (680 g) plums, pits removed and cut into ½-inch (12-mm) thick slices
½ cup (100 g) granulated sugar
1 tablespoon orange zest
1 tablespoon orange juice
½ teaspoon ground cinnamon
Pinch of kosher salt
1 tablespoon vanilla extract
2 tablespoons cornstarch
1 large egg, beaten with 1 tablespoon heavy cream
Turbinado sugar
Vanilla ice cream

To make the pie dough: Preheat the oven to 375°F (190°C).

In the bowl of a food processor, combine the flour, granulated sugar, and salt and pulse to combine. Add the butter and pulse until the butter is the size of peas. Add 3 tablespoons ice-cold water and pulse until the dough starts to pull away from the sides of the machine. If the dough is dry, add 1 tablespoon ice-cold water and pulse until the dough stays together when pinched with your fingers. Transfer the dough to a work surface and pat it into a disk. Cover with plastic wrap and refrigerate for at least 30 minutes or overnight.

To make the filling: In a large bowl, combine the plum slices, granulated sugar, orange zest, orange juice, cinnamon, salt, and vanilla and gently stir to combine. Add the cornstarch and gently stir to combine.

To prepare the galette: On a floured surface, roll the pie dough into a round about 12 inches (30.5 cm) in diameter and ⅛ inch (3 mm) thick. Transfer to a piece of parchment paper. Pile the plum mixture into the center of the dough round, leaving a 2-inch (5-cm) border. Fold the edges of the pie dough up and over the plum filling, pleating as you go. Brush the edges of the galette with egg wash and sprinkle with turbinado sugar.

Transfer the galette into the oven and bake for 45 to 50 minutes, until the crust is golden brown. Remove the galette from the oven, place on a wire rack, and let cool completely. Top with vanilla ice cream and serve immediately.

Serves 8 | Total Time: 1 hour and 30 minutes
(Prep: 15. Cook: 45 to 50.)

Meyer Lemon Bars

As you probably figured out by now, I wasn't that adventurous of an eater growing up. Things just weirded me out, including desserts with fruit in them. I was just a cookie and brownie kind of girl until I hit my twenties. So even though my mom made lemon bars all the time—she and my sister love them—I just wasn't on board. Fast-forward to now, when I've finally learned what's what and haven't since met a sweet course I'm not into. I finally realized how gorgeously complex Meyer lemons are—floral and sweet and citrusy—and how delicious their curd is sitting on top of a buttery crust. So I added these bars into the rotation because I feel like I have to make up for lost time!

Ingredients

For the crust:

Nonstick cooking spray
¾ cup (1½ sticks/170 g) unsalted butter, at room temperature
⅓ cup (65 g) granulated sugar
⅓ cup (40 g) powdered sugar, plus more for dusting
2 teaspoons Meyer lemon zest
1¾ cups (220 g) all-purpose flour
¼ teaspoon kosher salt

For the lemon filling:

4 large eggs
2 cups (400 g) granulated sugar
2 tablespoons Meyer lemon zest
⅔ cup (165 ml) Meyer lemon juice
⅔ cup (80 g) all-purpose flour
¼ teaspoon kosher salt
Powdered sugar

To make the crust: Preheat the oven to 350°F (175°C). Line a 9 by 9-inch (23 by 23-cm) baking dish with parchment paper with 1 inch (2.5 cm) hanging over the sides. Spray with nonstick cooking spray.

In a stand mixer, combine the butter, granulated sugar, and powdered sugar and cream on medium speed until light and fluffy, 2 to 4 minutes. Add the lemon zest and mix until combined. Add the flour and salt and mix until just combined. Dump the flour mixture into the prepared pan, and with your hands, pat the dough into an even layer on the bottom of the pan. Bake the crust for 15 to 17 minutes, until light golden brown. Remove from the oven, place on a wire rack, and let cool completely, leaving the oven on.

To make the lemon filling: In a large bowl, whisk together the eggs, granulated sugar, lemon zest, and lemon juice until smooth. Fold in the flour and salt and mix to combine.

To assemble and bake: Gently pour the lemon filling over the crust. Bake the lemon bars for 30 to 35 minutes, until the filling is set and just barely starting to brown. Remove from the oven and place on a wire rack to cool completely.

Using the parchment hanging over the sides of the baking dish, remove the lemon bars. Cut into squares, dust with powdered sugar, and serve.

Serves 9 to 16 | Total Time: 1 hour (Prep: 15. Cook: 45.)

Gooey Chocolate Chip Cookie Squares

After I tested this recipe, I put it in the fridge to cool, and two hours later my husband and I were parked in front of the fridge with two forks, eating these straight out of the pan like there was no tomorrow. They are that good. As hard as it will be, do NOT skip the two-hour cooling period, because there's carry-over baking that will help everything firm up without overbaking (which would make the squares too hard). After that, the only thing between you and this dessert is a fork!

Ingredients

Nonstick cooking spray
1 cup (2 sticks/225 g) unsalted butter, melted
2 cups (440 g) light brown sugar
4 teaspoons vanilla extract
2 large eggs
2 cups (250 g) all-purpose flour
1 teaspoon baking powder
¼ teaspoon baking soda
1 cup (175 g) chocolate discs
½ teaspoon Maldon sea salt

Preheat the oven to 350°F (175°C). Spray a 9 by 9-inch (23 by 23-cm) baking pan with nonstick cooking spray and line it with parchment paper.

In a large bowl or stand mixer, combine the melted butter and brown sugar and mix with a wooden spoon or the paddle attachment for 1 minute, or until combined. Add the vanilla and eggs and mix, scraping down the sides of the bowl, until fully incorporated. Add the flour, baking powder, and baking soda and slowly mix until just combined. The batter will be a bit stiff, but that's normal. Fold in almost all of the chocolate discs, leaving a few for sprinkling on top.

Spoon the batter into the prepared baking pan, sprinkle with the remaining chocolate discs and Maldon sea salt, and transfer to the oven. Bake for 30 minutes. The top should be golden brown and still have a slight jiggle when gently shaken. Remove from the oven, place on a wire rack, and let cool for at least 2 hours before cutting and serving. If you want to speed up the cooling process, transfer to the fridge for 30 minutes and then slice and serve.

Serves 9 to 16 | Total Time: 2 hours and 35 minutes
(Prep: 5. Cook: 30.)

Lemon Curd *and* Strawberry Tart

There are only four components to this recipe, so they each need be at their best to make this dessert extra-special. The first is flaky homemade tart crust, which is totally worth taking on since the rest of this dessert is so simple. The second is the lemon curd, which hits just the right note between sweet and tart (and is impossible not to just eat with a spoon). Third is the perfect pillow of whipped cream, and fourth is the fresh strawberries scattered over the top. Buying the best, freshest ingredients will go a long way here.

Ingredients

For the tart crust:

1 large egg yolk
1 to 2 tablespoons ice-cold water
1 teaspoon vanilla extract
1¼ cups (155 g) all-purpose flour, plus more for rolling
2 tablespoons almond meal or finely ground almonds
3 tablespoons granulated sugar
¼ teaspoon kosher salt
½ cup (1 stick/115 g) cold unsalted butter, cut into ¼-inch (6-mm) cubes

For the lemon curd filling:

1 tablespoon lemon zest
1 cup (240 ml) fresh lemon juice
¼ cup (60 ml) honey
½ cup (100 g) granulated sugar
4 large eggs
2 large egg yolks
Pinch of kosher salt
¾ cup (1½ sticks/170 g) unsalted butter, cubed

For the topping:

2 cups (480 ml) heavy cream
¾ cup (95 g) powdered sugar
Cute strawberries

To make the tart crust: Preheat the oven to 375°F (190°C).

In a small bowl, whisk together the egg yolk, 1 tablespoon of the ice-cold water, and the vanilla.

In the bowl of a food processor, combine the flour, almond meal, granulated sugar, and salt and pulse to combine. Add the butter and pulse 10 times, or until the butter is the size of peas. Add the egg yolk mixture and pulse until combined, 10 to 15 pulses. If the dough is still dry and doesn't stick together when pinched with your fingers, add the remaining 1 tablespoon water and pulse it in.

Transfer the dough to a work surface and pat it into a rectangular disk. Cover in plastic wrap and refrigerate for at least 30 minutes or up to 3 hours.

On a well-floured surface, roll the dough into an 11 by 7-inch (28 by 17-cm) rectangle that is about ⅛-inch (3-mm) thick. Using the rolling pin, carefully transfer the dough to the tart pan. Gently press the dough into the tart pan, trim the edges, and prick with a fork. Freeze the pan for 10 minutes.

Top the tart dough with aluminum foil and place pie weights on top. Bake the tart shell for 15 to 18 minutes, then carefully remove the foil and pie weights and bake for another 5 minutes, or until golden brown. Remove from the oven and place on a wire rack to cool completely.

(recipe continues)

Reduce the oven temperature to 350°F (175°C).

To make the lemon curd filling: In a medium nonreactive saucepan, whisk together the lemon zest, lemon juice, honey, granulated sugar, eggs, egg yolks, and salt. Place over medium heat and heat, whisking constantly, until the mixture is very thick, 5 to 7 minutes. Press the curd through a fine-mesh strainer into a bowl, then fold in the butter.

Pour the lemon curd into the tart shell, smoothing the surface so it's even, and bake for 30 minutes, or until barely set and the center jiggles slightly. Remove from the oven and place on a wire rack to cool completely. You could also refrigerate the tart for 1½ hours after removing it from the oven to cool it more quickly.

To make the topping and serve: In the bowl of a stand mixer, whip the cream with the powdered sugar until soft peaks form. Spread the whipped cream over the top of the tart, leaving parts of the lemon curd showing. Scatter with cute strawberries and serve.

Serves 6 to 8 | Total Time: At least 1 hour and 45 minutes (Prep: 10. Cook: 55.)

PRO
BLENDER

Chapter 10:

The Essentials: Vinaigrettes, Sauces, Dips + Spreads

This chapter may be last, but it's probably the most important one in the book. If you can make a great sauce, then you can turn pretty much anything into an incredible meal. Plus, a well-balanced sauce can also be a dip, marinade, spread, schmear, drizzle, dressing—you name it! These recipes are super-simple to make, easy to store, and put just about anything store-bought to shame.

Basil Vinaigrette

This dressing is my pride and joy, and I probably eat about a gallon of it a week—no joke. It's fresh and bright and works with just about everything: on a salad, tossed with pasta or grains, drizzled on fish or shrimp (it's particularly yummy with salmon), and slathered on a piece of avocado toast.

Ingredients

1 shallot, roughly chopped
2 cups (80 g) tightly packed fresh basil leaves
1 clove garlic, peeled
½ teaspoon red pepper flakes
½ cup (120 ml) olive oil
2 tablespoons red wine vinegar
1 teaspoon kosher salt, or to taste
Freshly cracked black pepper

In a high-powered blender, combine the shallot, basil, garlic, red pepper flakes, oil, vinegar, and salt and blend for 1 to 2 minutes, until very smooth. Add the salt and season with pepper. The dressing will keep in an airtight container in the fridge for up to 3 days.

Makes 1 cup (240 ml) | Total Time: 3 minutes

Tip: **Use this vinaigrette as dressing for a salad or cold pasta salad; as a marinade for steak, chicken, or veggies; drizzled on a savory tart; tossed with roasted veggies; or slathered on grilled corn.**

Balsamic Vinaigrette

This is the secret ingredient to Mom's Every Night Cucumber Salad (page 96) and a good part of the reason I lick the bowl clean every time I make it. I make a triple batch of this dressing every week and use it for lunches and dinners on the regular. It's not only great for spooning over veggies but perks up grains, salads, and most fish and meat dishes, and it works as a marinade, too.

Ingredients

¼ cup (60 ml) olive oil
3 tablespoons balsamic vinegar
3 cloves garlic, chopped
1 shallot, finely chopped
1 teaspoon herbes de Provence
Kosher salt and freshly cracked black pepper to taste

In a small bowl, whisk together all the ingredients. Adjust the salt and pepper as needed. The dressing will keep in an airtight container in the fridge for up to 1 week.

Makes ½ cup (120 ml) | Total Time: 2 minutes

Cilantro Vinaigrette

One of the most popular recipes that I ever put on my blog was my Basil Vinaigrette (opposite). People went nuts for how it added the perfect pop of acidity to just about anything. This is the same basic recipe but calls for cilantro instead of basil, which has the same all-purpose versatility but with more of a Tex-Mex vibe.

Ingredients

1 shallot, roughly chopped
2 cups (80 g) tightly packed fresh cilantro leaves
1 or 2 cloves garlic, peeled
½ teaspoon red pepper flakes
½ cup (120 ml) olive oil
2 tablespoons red wine vinegar
1 teaspoon kosher salt, or to taste
Freshly cracked black pepper

In a high-powered blender, combine the shallot, cilantro, garlic, red pepper flakes, oil, vinegar, and salt. Blend for 1 to 2 minutes, until very smooth. Adjust the salt as needed and season with pepper. The dressing will keep in an airtight container in the fridge for up to 3 days.

Makes 1 cup (240 ml) | Total Time: 3 minutes

Lemon-Champagne Vinaigrette

One of my best friends and culinary partner in crime, Minka, always makes this epic salad dressing. It's so fresh and light and yet somehow makes everything taste like a better version of itself. You can substitute red wine vinegar for the champagne vinegar and it'll still be just as tasty.

Ingredients

Juice of 1 lemon
1 tablespoon champagne vinegar
2 cloves garlic, finely chopped
1 shallot, finely chopped
⅓ cup (75 ml) olive oil
Kosher salt and freshly cracked black pepper to taste

Combine all the ingredients in a small bowl and whisk to combine. Adjust the salt and pepper as needed. The dressing will keep in an airtight container in the fridge for up to 5 days.

Makes ⅔ cup (165 ml) | Total Time: 2 minutes

Mustard-Herb Vinaigrette

Homemade dressings are one of the most important elements in my pantry. Using them is the easiest way to change up your usual rotation and add a ton of flavor to otherwise simple ingredients. If I make a big grilled romaine salad, switching up the dressing is the easiest way to get excited about a few days of leftovers. Or drizzle some into a bowl of rice and all of a sudden it has way more personality. Plus, they're all super-simple to make—nothing you can't just whisk together in a bowl or buzz in a blender.

This dressing is a multipurpose all-star. Use it to marinate steak or chicken before grilling, slather it on some roasted sweet potatoes, mix it into a bed of farro with some thinly sliced veggies, or use it to add a little zest to an otherwise plain side salad.

Ingredients

2 cloves garlic, minced
1 shallot, minced
2 tablespoons grainy Dijon mustard
2 teaspoons dried oregano
2 teaspoons dried parsley
½ teaspoon freshly cracked black pepper
½ teaspoon kosher salt
¼ cup (60 ml) red wine vinegar
1¼ cups (300 ml) olive oil
2 tablespoons finely shredded Parmesan cheese (optional)

Combine all the ingredients in small bowl and whisk until everything is incorporated. Store in an airtight container in the refrigerator for up to 1 week.

Makes 1½ cups (360 ml) | Total Time: 3 minutes

Homemade BBQ Sauce

I'm pretty sure I don't have to sell you on how tasty really good barbecue sauce is. The beauty of making it yourself is that you can not only tailor it to your taste, but you also end up with one that doesn't have a ton of extra sugar like the packaged versions do. Because it stores for a long time in the fridge, I highly recommend keeping some on hand for tossing with pulled pork, drizzling over any kind of protein, or using as a dipping sauce the same way you would ketchup.

Ingredients

1 tablespoon olive oil
¾ cup (85 g) chopped yellow onion
2 cloves garlic, minced
1 cup (165 g) chopped mango
½ cup (120 ml) tomato sauce
2 tablespoons packed brown sugar
2 tablespoons Worcestershire sauce
2 tablespoons balsamic vinegar
1 canned chipotle chile in adobo sauce, plus 1 tablespoon adobo sauce
Kosher salt

In a medium saucepan, heat the oil over medium-high heat. Add the onion and garlic and cook for 2 to 3 minutes, until softened and fragrant.

Add the mango, tomato sauce, brown sugar, Worcestershire sauce, vinegar, chipotle chile, and adobo sauce and bring to a boil. Reduce the heat and simmer, uncovered, for 15 to 18 minutes, until thickened. Remove from the heat and let cool slightly (don't blend it while it's super-hot).

Transfer to a blender or food processor and blend until smooth. Season with salt. The sauce will keep in an airtight container in the fridge for up to 3 weeks.

Makes 2 cups (480 ml) | Total Time: 30 minutes
(Prep: 10. Cook: 20.)

Tip: **Try BBQ sauce with French fries; as a dunking option for grilled cheese; tossed with roasted or grilled chicken and quinoa for a BBQ chicken salad; on a burger; as a pizza or flatbread sauce; or as cooking liquid for braised pork shoulder.**

Charred Corn Salsa

This California Girl can never get enough salsa, so here's another one to add to the mix. I love combining charred corn with poblanos and jalapeños for that sweet, smoky, and spicy effect.

Ingredients

1 poblano pepper
4 or 5 ears corn on the cob
2 teaspoons olive oil
1 jalapeño chile, finely chopped
½ small red onion, finely chopped
2 tablespoons chopped fresh chives
Zest and juice of 1 lime
Kosher salt and freshly cracked black pepper

Preheat a charcoal or gas grill to medium-high heat.

Brush the poblano pepper and corn with the oil. Place the vegetables over the grill and grill until they develop grill marks, turning occasionally, 5 to 6 minutes total. Remove from the grill and let cool.

Peel the skin away from the poblano pepper and finely chop the flesh. Carefully remove the corn kernels from the cob and transfer both vegetables to a large bowl. Add the jalapeño, red onion, chives, and lime zest and juice and season with salt and pepper. Serve immediately, or place in an airtight container and refrigerate for up to 3 days.

Makes 1½ cups (360 ml) | Total Time: 10 minutes
(Prep: 5. Cook: 5.)

Pineapple-Mango Salsa

Tropical salsas are the easiest way to punch up a dish. I especially love this one on fish, particularly fish tacos. Then, of course, you can also have it with chips and guac.

Ingredients

2 cups (330 g) diced fresh pineapple
1 cup (165 g) diced mango
½ cup (65 g) finely diced red onion
3 scallions, green parts only, thinly sliced
2 tablespoons finely chopped red jalapeño chile
2 tablespoons chopped fresh cilantro
1 tablespoon chopped fresh chives
1 tablespoon fresh lime juice
Kosher salt and freshly cracked black pepper

In a medium bowl, combine the pineapple, mango, red onion, scallions, jalapeño, cilantro, chives, and lime juice. Toss to combine and season with salt and pepper. Refrigerate the salsa for 30 minutes before serving. It will keep in an airtight container in the refrigerator for up to 3 days.

Makes 3 cups (565 g) | Total Time: 5 minutes

Tomatillo-Avocado Salsa

My favorite green salsa with avocado whipped in—a total win. It's as good for dipping as it is for drizzling.

Ingredients

1 pound (455 g) medium tomatillos
1 small yellow onion, quartered
½ jalapeño chile (remove the seeds if you want, or leave them in for an extra kick)
3 cloves garlic
1 tablespoon honey
1 bunch fresh cilantro, stems removed and discarded, leaves roughly chopped
1 ripe avocado, pitted, flesh scooped out, peel discarded
Zest and juice of 1 lime
Kosher salt and freshly cracked black pepper

Preheat the oven to 450°F (230°C).

Remove the husks from the tomatillos, rinse the tomatillos under warm water, and wipe them clean. Cut the tomatillos in half and place them on a baking pan along with the onion and jalapeño. Roast for 20 minutes, or until softened. Remove from the oven and set aside to cool.

Combine all the ingredients in a food processor and pulse for 1 to 2 minutes, until smooth and creamy, adding a little water if needed until the salsa is smooth like salad dressing. Adjust the salt and pepper as needed. The salsa will keep in an airtight container in the refrigerator for up to 1 week.

Makes 2 cups (480 ml) | Total Time: 25 minutes
(Prep: 5. Cook: 20.)

Tip: **Use salsa as braising liquid for slow-cooked chicken thighs; added to scrambled eggs; on top of a burger; as pizza or flatbread sauce; heaped on a grain bowl; instead of enchilada sauce; folded into mac 'n' cheese; inside burritos or tacos, naturally; on top of roasted fish; or loaded on a baked potato.**

Homemade Chipotle Ketchup

Ketchup was one of the few food groups I ate growing up, and I still love this condiment like no other. I put it on everything—eggs, grilled cheese, burgers, fries, hot dogs . . . the list goes on. This version has just a little bit of kick and puts store-bought ketchup to shame.

Ingredients

2 tablespoons olive oil
1 medium onion, chopped
1 clove garlic, chopped
1 (28-ounce/840-ml) can tomato puree
½ cup (110 g) brown sugar
¼ cup (60 ml) apple cider vinegar
1 tablespoon tomato paste
1 to 2 chipotle chiles in adobo sauce
1 teaspoon kosher salt, or to taste
½ teaspoon ground mustard
½ teaspoon ground cayenne
¼ teaspoon ground allspice
⅛ teaspoon ground cloves

Heat the oil in a medium saucepan over medium heat. Add the onion and cook for 5 to 8 minutes, until translucent. Add the garlic and cook, stirring, for about 30 seconds, until fragrant. Add the tomato puree, brown sugar, vinegar, tomato paste, chipotles, salt, mustard, cayenne, allspice, and cloves and stir to combine. Increase the heat to high and bring to a boil, then reduce the heat to low and simmer, stirring occasionally, for 30 to 45 minutes, until the mixture is thick like ketchup.

Using an immersion blender, food processor, or standing blender, blend the mixture until smooth. (If you're using a standing blender, let the mixture cool for 15 to 20 minutes before blending.) Taste and adjust the salt as needed. Pour the ketchup into an airtight container, cover, and store in the refrigerator for up to 1 month.

Makes 2 cups (480 ml) | Total Time: 45 minutes
(Prep: 5. Cook: 40 to 50.)

Green *Goddess* Dip

A traditional green goddess is made with mayo and sour cream, but that's just not how this California Girl rolls. That said, I'm all about the creamy factor, so I use avocado instead and the final product is just as herbaceous and tangy as the original. Use it as a dip with veggies, make it into a dressing (loosened up with a bit more water, if necessary), or spread on your favorite sandwich.

Ingredients

1 medium ripe avocado, pitted, flesh scooped out, peel discarded
2 scallions, white and light green parts, roughly chopped
1 teaspoon lemon zest
2 tablespoons fresh lemon juice
2 tablespoons champagne vinegar
3 tablespoons water, plus more if needed
¼ cup (60 ml) extra-virgin olive oil
1 cup (40 g) roughly chopped fresh basil
⅓ cup (17 g) roughly chopped fresh flat-leaf parsley
¼ cup (11 g) snipped fresh chives
1 clove garlic, peeled
Kosher salt and freshly cracked black pepper to taste

In a food processor or high-powered blender, combine all the ingredients and process until smooth, adding more water if needed to smooth it out. Taste and adjust the salt and pepper as needed. Use immediately, or store in an airtight container in the refrigerator for up to 4 days.

Makes 2 cups (480 ml) | Total Time: 5 minutes

Salsa Verde

In addition to adding bold, herbaceous flavor to anything and everything (seriously—it's a one-stop shop for salad dressing, veggie dip, pasta sauce, marinade, chicken, fish, or meat-topper), this recipe is perfect for using up all those leftover herbs at the end of the week.

Ingredients

Leaves from 1 bunch fresh flat-leaf parsley
Leaves from 1 bunch fresh cilantro
20 fresh basil leaves
2 cloves garlic, peeled
2 tablespoons red wine vinegar
2 tablespoons capers, drained and rinsed
½ to ¾ cup (120 to 180 ml) olive oil
Kosher salt and freshly cracked black pepper

In a food processor, combine the parsley, cilantro, basil, garlic, vinegar, and capers and pulse until coarsely chopped, about 30 seconds. Transfer to a small bowl, stir in the oil, and season with salt and pepper. Store in an airtight container in the refrigerator for up to 5 days.

Makes 1 cup (165 ml) | Total Time: 3 minutes

Tip: **Try salsa verde on a crudité board; mixed with roasted potatoes; on a bruschetta bar; drizzled over any grilled protein; on top of eggs; with fried halloumi; mixed with avocado for a quick salsa; tossed into a pasta salad; spooned over grilled veggies; whipped with mayo for a sandwich spread; or as pizza or flatbread sauce.**

Saffron Tomato Confit

Okay, I know I say that a lot of things are life-changing, but I've seriously been making this recipe on repeat since my best friend's best friend—basically my best friend by association—Dana Robinson introduced me to the idea of taking those tomatoes that have been sitting on your counter for just a tad too long—you know the ones!—and turning them into the richest, jammiest yumminess. It's basically cherry tomatoes that are slowly simmered in lots of good-quality olive oil along with some saffron, salt, and pepper. That's it. Could it get any easier? I eat this on just about everything: toasted pita bread? Yes. Grilled bread with a schmear of fresh ricotta cheese? Yes. Chicken, salmon, or beef? Yes. Quinoa, farro, risotto? Yes, yes, and yes! Are you sensing a pattern? Hop to it!

Ingredients

1 pound (455 g) cherry tomatoes, halved
⅓ cup (75 ml) good-quality olive oil
Pinch of saffron (about 20 threads)
Kosher salt and freshly cracked black pepper

In a medium skillet, combine the tomatoes, oil, saffron, and a pinch of salt and pepper. Place over medium-high heat and heat until the tomatoes start to blister, about 10 minutes. Reduce the heat to medium-low and simmer for about 1 hour, stirring every 10 minutes, until the tomatoes start falling apart.

Remove the pan from the heat and cool for about 20 minutes, adjust the salt and pepper as needed, and serve with grilled bread if you like. The confit will keep in an airtight container in the refrigerator for up to 1 week. Let it come to room temperature before serving.

Makes 2 cups (480 ml) | Total Time: 1 hour and 35 minutes (Prep: 5. Cook: 1 hour and 10 minutes.)

Tip: **Use tomato sauce or slow-cooked tomatoes with pasta or cooked grains; simmered with eggs until the whites are set; poured over meatballs; in chicken or eggplant Parmesan; drizzled on bread; or as pizza or flatbread sauce.**

Acknowledgments

This book would not be complete without a massive and heartfelt thank you to the people who made it possible.

First and foremost, enormous gratitude to every single person who has been a part of the What's Gaby Cooking family. From my dedicated blog readers, to my Instagram and Snapchat family, and everyone else in between, I am forever grateful for you. You bring so much joy into my life, and without you, none of this would be possible.

To Matt Armendariz and Adam Pearson—without you guys, this book simply wouldn't exist—or if it did, it wouldn't be nearly as beautiful. Thank you for helping me make What's Gaby Cooking into what it is today, for letting me march around the studio with a clipboard, pretending to be in charge, for entertaining my insane cheese board and loaded salad ideas, and for being the best friends a girl could ask for. Three Musketeers for life.

To Amy Paliwoda, for being the best prop stylist I could ever dream up! I never want to have a party without your styling fairy dust ever again. Thank you for capturing the California Girl vibe in every moment.

To Holly Dolce, for understanding what makes me tick—and letting me run with it! Working on this book with you has been a dream come true.

To Janis Donnaud, for being the most fearless and bad-ass agent ever. Thank you for telling it like it is, not sugarcoating anything, and for standing next to me every step of the way.

To Byron, Laura Ford, Hristina, Sophie, and Elizabeth for working tirelessly on all the photo shoots and for being willing to gain ten (okay maybe fifteen) pounds with me in two weeks while we ate every single recipe in this book.

To Rachel Holtzman, thank you for being so incredible and zoning in on what it feels like to be a California Girl!

To Simone, for teaching me how to entertain in true California Girl style (without breaking a sweat) and welcoming me into your family when I moved to LA. And to Phine, Frankie, and Allegra, for being down to try anything I made (within reason). You all mean the world to me.

To everyone who helped make this book even more beautiful: Fifty One and a Half (the most stunning handmade ceramics ever created), FarmLot 59, Williams-Sonoma, Anthropologie, Erica Cloud, and Lynn Simpson! You guys rock.

To everyone on the What's Gaby Cooking team, past and present. Lily, Hilary, Raina, Karen, Reesa, Emily, Alix, and Micki—thank you!

To my friends both near and far who I can always count on to come over and taste test my recipes, show up for photo shoots disguised as parties, let me intrude on their kitchens when I need a change of scenery, and brainstorm recipe ideas in the middle of a phone call. You are all my most favorite people to cook for, and I love you guys so much.

To my mom, dad, and sister: For cheering me on for as long as I can remember. I wouldn't be who I am today without your constant love, support, and guidance. Thank you for instilling in me the confidence, fearlessness, and motivation that has allowed me to follow my dreams.

And last, but certainly not least, to my husband, Thomas: For allowing me to be me, and for being the best partner I could ever imagine. I love you more than words can describe, forever.

index

Note: Page numbers in *italics* indicate photos.

D

E

F

G